James Payn

Cecil's Tryst

Vol. 1

James Payn

Cecil's Tryst
Vol. 1

ISBN/EAN: 9783337346478

Printed in Europe, USA, Canada, Australia, Japan

Cover: Foto ©Thomas Meinert / pixelio.de

More available books at **www.hansebooks.com**

𝔄 𝔑𝔬𝔳𝔢𝔩.

BY THE AUTHOR OF

'LOST SIR MASSINGBERD,' 'A PERFECT TREASURE,'
'LIKE FATHER, LIKE SON,' ETC.

IN THREE VOLUMES.

VOL. I.

LONDON:

TINSLEY BROTHERS, 18 CATHERINE ST. STRAND.

1872.

LONDON:
ROBSON AND SONS, PRINTERS, PANCRAS ROAD, N.W.

This Book

IS CORDIALLY DEDICATED TO

Mrs. WALFORD

BY HER FRIEND THE AUTHOR.

CONTENTS OF VOL. I.

CECIL'S TRYST.

CHAPTER I.

GATCOMBE.

IF you know the south country, you must
needs have heard of the Wrays of Gatcombe.
They represented Sandylandshire for three
successive parliaments, and ruined themselves in endeavouring to do so in the
fourth, in the teeth of Fate and the Reform
Bill. It used to be a boast of the race that
none of them had ever accepted subordinate
political office—and no high one was ever
offered to them, for they had not good
brains—nor a title from a minister. They

would have been peers if they could, perhaps; but to have been Sir Frederick Wray,
Bart., would have been to be the last of a
third-rate order; while to be Fred. Wray of
Gatcombe, was to be the first of Sandylandshire notables. The head of the house was
always a Frederick, and the name was ab-
breviated by the country-folk for love—if
the affectionate regards of a constituency
can be so entitled. When the Wrays lost
their seat and their 'position,' they began
to be intellectual. The first who inaugu-
rated this regime was my father.

His younger brother, Thomas, was also
a clever fellow in a very different line. He
was a soldier of fortune; which, in those
days, meant a soldier who had the art of
acquiring other people's fortunes — mostly
those of the natives of India. He quitted
home, to open the Hindustan oyster with
his sword, before I came into the world, and
never saw the white cliffs of England again:
so Uncle Tom and I never met. As a

memory, however, he had more substanti-
ality in my eyes than many whom I have
been acquainted with in the flesh. When I
was a boy of ten, his doings had not died
out of mind in the county yet, and the re-
cital of them interested me amazingly. His
feats at election-time—the election that had
ruined us all—had, in particular, quite a
magical attraction for me. If pluck, and
straight hitting from the shoulder, could
have won my father his seat, the partisan-
ship of Uncle Tom would have secured it
for him; he drove about with the gold in
bags, and sowed it broadcast; he spoke, in
public, such words against our adversary as
(at that time) invited pistol-shots, and they
were welcome to him; he 'neutralised'
five-and-twenty adverse votes by standing
throughout the poll-day at the head of the
cellar-stairs at the Red Lion, at Lipton, with
a shutter-bar in his hand, and daring the
imprisoned ' free and independent' to 'come
on.' When a ' dead lift' was necessary, our

agent said that there was no man that could be so thoroughly depended upon as Mr. Tom. My grandmother had Irish blood in her veins, which, it was said, accounted for it. But notwithstanding this charitable view of his character—which was, after all, only taken by our own side, the losing one—and the warm affection that existed between the brothers, I think it was rather a relief to my father when Tom went to expend his superfluous energies in India. It was whispered that there was some difficulty in getting him off; not that he didn't wish to go, but that he was 'wanted' by the police in respect to some frivolous and vexatious charge, to answer which might, nevertheless, have delayed him for some years. Indeed, it was to avoid this troublesome matter that he never came home again.

After our political fiasco, my father retired into private life, which, indeed, the crippled state of his finances would have compelled him to do at any rate; but the fact was, he was by nature inclined for study and seclusion. He had few sympathies in common with those of the county families about him. He was no sportsman; would never even have preserved his game, had it not been for my uncle's sake, in whose eyes a pheasant was, what few other objects were, a sacred thing; and when he did ride, he rode cobs. At the time I speak of, there was but one even of those humble animals in the great stables at Gatcombe, formerly so well filled with champing steeds; though, afterwards (as you shall hear), we did increase our stud a little. The home establishment, generally, was upon a very limited scale, considering the size of the house itself, which was very great. Under its roof the Wrays had lived and died for centuries, and my father clung to it in his fallen fortunes: otherwise I don't think he cared very much about being called Fred. Wray of Gatcombe, nor, indeed, for fame at all, though it were of a much less questionable sort. If he prided himself on anything, it was on his philosophy. He was a scholar of a very rare kind; not in Greek or Latin—though he was not ignorant of those languages— but in old English literature, chiefly of the Elizabethan era. The drama of that period was his especial delight. He knew all Shakespeare, I verily believe, by heart; but his favourite quotations were from the contemporaries of our great National Poet, such as Greene and Marlowe, Dekker and Webster, the application of whose lines to modern circumstances sounded in unlearned ears absurdly enough, and somewhat weirdly also. The first recollections I have of my father—with his pointed Vandyck beard, and in the long red dressing-gown which was his usual wear till mid-day, sonorously reciting from the old playwrights—are those of a kindly magician. No poet ever imagined a kindlier soul, though it was his humour to hide his tenderness behind a thin veil of banter. One practice, in particular, he adopted from one of his favourite authors, namely, the addressing of those he loved best by the most unloving titles; thus, I have heard him call Aunt Ben 'Sycorax;' and even, on one occasion, when he wished to be specially affectionate, 'Thou Stygian Witch,' which sounded very surprisingly to a stranger. Aunt Ben was my maiden aunt, Miss Benita Wray, who presided over the household, and had done so ever since my mother's death, which happened in my infancy. She had the utmost respect for my father, and understood him thoroughly, though without attempting to enter into his pursuits. Her literature, indeed, was confined to the titles of the jam-pots in the preserve cupboard, with one remarkable exception. She was so assiduous a student of the Bible, and gifted with so marvellous a memory, that she could give chapter and verse for every text. In this accomplishment of Aunt Ben's my father took especial pride, and was for ever endeavouring to confound her.

Gatcombe Manor—for the house still went by its old name, though the manor had passed into other hands than ours—was a huge rectangular building, of no particular style, the design of which (if its architect had ever had any) seemed to have been to enclose a space in its centre, called 'the Court,' into which half the bedroom windows looked, to the great depression of their tenants' spirits. It was paved, and had a draw-well in it, which my infant mind associated with the wicked doings of little Bobby Greene. 'Did you *know* Bobby Greene, papa,' I once inquired, 'who drowned the poor cat?'

'I knew him well,' answered my father gravely.

'Was it a tortoise-shell,' said I pathetically, 'like ours?'

'It was buxom, and blithe, and young, I ween,
Beauteous like a summer's queen;

For her sides were ruddy hued,
As if lilies were imbrued
With drops of blood, to make the white
Please the eye with more delight.'

Then, to stop the tears set flowing by this
tender picture, he added—still felicitously
quoting from even an older Bobby Greene
than mine :

' Weep not, my wanton ; smile upon my knee ;
When thou art old, there's grief enough for thee.'

And thus, from my earliest years, was
I regaled with tags and snatches of old
verse, till they grew as familiar as nursery
rhymes.

My father had a rooted antipathy to all
schools, derived, I fancy, from some unpleasant personal experience of them, and
educated me himself at home. When any
remonstrance was made with him on this
account—which was but seldom, for there
were few who had the right to interfere in
such a matter, and fewer still who cared to
' tackle' him upon any subject on which he

was known to have a prejudice—he had this cut-and-dry reply: 'If my boy lives, he will know more that is worth knowing than your prize school-prig; and if he dies, he will at least have had a happy boyhood.' The latter part of this statement I can honestly corroborate. I had a pony of my own, plenty of pocket-money, and a leaping-pole, the charms of which last are, I notice, almost unknown to the boys of to-day. At twelve, though a tall boy, I could clear my own height with ease; while as for breadth, there was scarce a brook in the county that I could not fly over like a bird. The pole, strong, supple, and light, was at least ten feet long; and with its help, I could go across country, taking a far straighter line as to fences than the best hunter that my ancestors had ever crossed. Many a time, from the steep bank of some Sandylandshire lane, have I cleared a returning team with their astonished guardian; flocks of sheep; and even on one occasion a herd of oxen.

The buoyant spring, the hurtling through the air, the thud of my young feet upon the opposite bank, recur to me as I write, and stir the sluggish blood within me even now. Independently of this accomplishment, the country round had its peculiar charms for a wholesome-minded lad, which, thanks to my father, I think I was. Behind and above the house, though it was built on high ground, stretched an immense tableland of wind-swept heath, the soil of which was finest sand. This was a paradise for rabbits. Moreover, there were a thousand caverns, for the whole place was honeycombed for the sake of the scythe-stones which it yielded. For generations it had thus been undermined, and the work was going on still. One result of this was to form from the excavations a magnificent terrace, miles and miles in length, the view from which extended over half-a-dozen counties, and even, at some points, to the ocean. The eyes of Columbus could hardly

have feasted upon the Land of the West
with greater delight than mine did upon
that fringe of sea, to which in those days I
never approached nearer. The sighing of
the fir-trees, that grew in great profusion
on the sand-cliff, did duty more efficiently
than I was aware of for the unheard murmur of the waves. I can hear them now,
and smell their sweet pungent breath,
which the wise men of to-day aver to be a
specific against consumption. It was not
so, however, in my time, for consumption
was the scourge of Gatcombe. Not that
the village was itself unhealthy, but that
almost the whole population, men, women,
and children, worked in the scythe-stone
caverns, and thereby destroyed themselves.

It was impossible to persuade them to
do otherwise, because the gains of that
employment were so much greater than
what could be earned in agricultural labour. All day long, through summer and
winter, the stroke of the spade and the

click of the hammer mingled with the murmur of the firs, that shook their funereal heads above this scene, as though in sorrowful protest. Scores of men were at work, each in his own burrow—the right to dig in which for his private behoof he purchased—like bees in the cells of some huge comb; and the women and children helped, by wheeling out the sand in barrows, and emptying them on the terrace. Their husbands and fathers, working in an unventilated space, where there was scarcely room to turn, were in a manner digging their own tombs. At home, it was the women's task to shape the stone thus obtained into the form of that with which 'the mower whets his scythe;' and they, too, were working for the mower Death, for the thin particles of dust that escaped during the process into the lungs were sooner or later fatal to them. Thus it happened that there was scarcely an old man or an old woman in all the village.

By a boy, however, such social calamities are ill understood, if understood at all.
There was, in fact, to my mind something
attractive in our people, and which con-
trasted very favourably with the looks of
other villagers; and it was long before I
came to know that the bright eyes and
high-coloured cheeks about us meant dis-
ease, and the absence of old people the
king of terrors. Moreover, there was no
want at Gatcombe, for the work, such as
it was, was plentiful, and well paid; while
melancholy was a thing unknown (at least
as a public spectacle), for the motto of the
toilers was, 'A short life and a merry one,'
and their cares they drowned in cider.

My father and Aunt Ben did what they
could to amend this state of things; in particular, certain masks were purchased for
the women to wear during their hurtful
toil; and if little good was effected (the
children used to play at highwaymen, I
remember, in the masks), their endeavours   •

were appreciated, even by those who declined to take advantage of them. After
all, I have forgotten to mention the chief
peril of the sand-cliff, and which invested
it in my boyish eyes with a ghastly interest.
There was scarcely one of these narrow
caves but had its catastrophe. A man could
not pay the sum, small as it was, that was
necessary to buy fir-poles for the support
of his cell walls; or (which was more common) he would dispose of them for drink;
whence it sooner or later happened that
some stroke of his pickaxe brought down
a fall of sand on his devoted head, or, worse,
brought it down behind him, so as to set
an impassable barrier between himself and
the world without. It was then of small
avail, even though another were working
near him, to give the alarm; for tons upon
tons of sand were often brought down,
through which the would-be rescuers had
to dig, propping and roofing their way at
every step, lest they also should share the

fate of the victim. The disaster was so
common, that everything was done at once
—though almost always in vain—to avert
the catastrophe. A messenger was dis-
patched on horseback for a surgeon; and
in the mean time my father was summoned,
who, with Aunt Ben, would hurry to the
spot with blankets, brandy, and a lancet.
It was long before I was permitted to be a
witness of such a scene; but I knew a score
of places where the tragedy had occurred,
and had its details at my finger-ends. Sometimes a family would still work on in a
cave that had actually been the living tomb
of their progenitor, and even neglect those
very precautions, the lack of which had
proved fatal to him : such contempt can
familiarity breed of even death itself. Not
a ghost haunted the hill. The fate of those
who perished there was held as natural as
that which carried others to the churchyard
by a more tedious route; just as soldiers
on service regard death upon the battle-'7

field as no more strange than in the hospital ward.

The wholesome air of high-placed Gatcombe discouraged all morbid ideas; on the hottest July day there was always a breeze upon the heath, a gentle swaying of the pine-tops. The woods themselves were dowered with an eternal beauty. In winter, they did not lose their green; in summer, the layers of shade above kept off the heat, while beneath, at each tree-foot, was spread a carpet of moss, in which one's limbs sank till they were hid. What bliss to lie on such, and watch through the green roof the clouds sail slowly by, or, twixt the straight red stems, that fair expanse of hill and plain, the apple-orchards, the low white farms, the streams and copses, and, in the western verge, the tall gray towers of Monkton, the cathedral town! They were too far to make their iron tongue be heard; the wood-pigeons' coo overhead alone broke the summer silence. That happy time

went by unnoted, the hours of which recur
with such sombre clang to-day—the knell
of the unburied Past.　O youth, youth,
youth! if ever thou comest back to us
again, then indeed there is a Heaven!

In my early days, I had no playmate
save the village boys, and many a rough
game and rougher combat did I have with
them.　There was one amusement that was
an especial favourite.　The sand-cliff sloped
on all sides, affording the softest falling:
and to run and leap out into the air as
far as possible, and to fall and fall, was a
glorious pastime.　To the stranger, such
experiments appeared suicidal—a leap from
the Tarpeian rock; but they were free
from danger, unless one disinhumed oneself
from one's sand-grave too tardily, and the
next cleaver of the air fell, Icarus-like, upon
one's head and shoulders.　Before this
sport all others paled; it was sublime—
epic.

If I had no boy-companion, I had a

friend of the gentler sex in Eleanor Bourne,
the vicar's daughter. She was called the
Gipsy, from her dark complexion, but might
have been termed so almost as fitly from
the out-of-door life she led. I, too, loved
'to hear the lark sing rather than the
mouse squeak,' and grudged every moment
of sunshine that found me within walls;
but I had my father's teaching to attend
to, whereas Nelly pursued even her studies
in the open air. How often have I found
her—not by accident—sitting at a pine-foot,
with her black hair, through which she
would nevertheless contrive to spy me
coming, falling over the pages of *Télémaque*,
and with a whole library of educational
works beside her, which were moved to
make room for me. Like me, she was
motherless; but there all similarity in our
circumstances ceased. Her father was a
conventional parson; had taken moderate
honours at the university; was grave and
dull; and fancied, because he was pompous,

that he was impressive. It seemed to me
that he had somehow missed being a gentleman; but perhaps that was prejudice on
my part. His father, who was still alive,
and lived at the vicarage, had purchased
much of the land with which the Wrays
had had to part; and the mind of a boy
is prone to resent what a man's judgment
acquiesces in. But as for Mr. Bourne the
elder, he had missed being a gentleman by
a mile — one of those mushroom men, of
whom it has been so happily said, that their
being 'self-made' relieves the Creator from
a very grave responsibility. How thoroughly would my father, with his deep
sense of humour, have appreciated that remark; but in those days American satire
had not shot its sharp beams across the
sea.

Nelly and I were fast friends and constant companions — lovers, if you will,
though the love was of a very innocent
sort, and unsuspected even by ourselves.

We read together; talked and thought over many a rich volume borrowed from my father's shelves; and I suppose, considering our Platonic passion, and the nature of our studies, we may have been set down as 'blue.' We knew not of the term, however, except as the colour of the sky, that ever roofed those youthful days. Undimmed by cloud, unvexed by storm, it stretched above us, until an event occurred which was fated to bring me face to face with the world, and to make the past appear a page from some *Life in Dreamland.* Perhaps I have already dwelt on it too long; as one who, leaning o'er her harp, dwells on some tune, of which her hearers tire, but which in *her* ears discourses sweetest melody, because it wakes the thought of bygone days.

CHAPTER II.

THE letters used to arrive at Gatcombe about breakfast - time ; and the 'Manor bag,' as the postman called it, was generally brought in during the discussion of that meal, and opened by my father, not quite so promptly as Aunt Ben desired. Women never tire of receiving letters ; whereas men, after middle life, for the most part abhor them. *They* do not write for the sake of interchanging gossip, 'keeping up' old friendship, or with 'effusion' of any kind. Business and bills form the staple of their correspondence ; and though the day of bills—and it had been a bitter one—was past in my father's case, business always troubled him ; that is, the

mere details of it, though he had plenty
of sagacity, and was practical enough
whenever he gave himself the trouble to
be so. He had a contempt and dislike
for the management of affairs, which those
who did not know him might easily have
mistaken for affectation. 'A good man
of business,' he would aver, was a man
who was good for nothing else ; and 'common sense was exactly what the term implied — no more, no less — the average
sagacity, not to possess which was to be
beneath the ordinary intellectual standard.'
Conventional opinions to the contrary, em-
bodied in such expressions as, 'He has
every sense but common sense,' and applied to men of genius, irritated him exceedingly. 'The meaning these idiots
intend to convey, I suppose, is, that men
of genius are blind to their own advantage ; whereas the fact is that they do not
find their advantage where the dolts do,
otherwise they would attain the same ob-

jects with far greater ease.' Perhaps my
father had been twitted with this supposed
deficiency himself. He certainly did not
like the Manor bag, and opened it upon
this particular occasion with the usual
tardiness and careless contempt. The expression of his face altered a little, however, as he drew forth an Indian letter,
and turned it over unopened in his hand.

'A letter from Tom!' cried my aunt.
'Well, I'm sure it's about time he wrote:
we have not heard from him for years.'

'It's not from Tom,' said my father
gravely.

'I trust nothing has gone wrong with
him?' continued Aunt Ben with agitation.

'I trust not,' was my father's answer.
There was a grim solemnity in his tone,
which I knew augured the worst. 'Go to
the study, my boy,' said he, laying his
hand affectionately on my head; 'I have
a few words for your aunt's private ear.'

When my father entered his sanctum,

half an hour afterwards, he wore a black coat in place of his red dressing-gown; from which I gathered at once that my Uncle Tom was dead; which was the case.

'You have lost an uncle, my boy, whom you have never seen; but I an only brother, who was at one time all in all to me. True, that was long ago: circumstances occurred to estrange us, even before he left England, and we have not met these thirty years; but—'

There was a portrait of my uncle in the study, painted when he was a very young man: it showed a face of great beauty and fire, but without the tenderness which was the charm of his brother's less handsome features. My father's eye here lit on this; he stopped midway in his speech, and rising, approached the picture with reverent looks. 'Dear Tom,' said he, with inexpressible pathos, 'goodbye; your last wishes shall be obeyed, just as though I had been beside your

deathbed and heard them.' He sighed,
returned to his chair, and then addressed
me in tones that were serious, but no
longer sad.

'The best tribute one can pay to the
memory of the dead, my dear boy, is to
respect their injunctions : all the trappings
and suits of woe are not worth a dump.
The next best thing is to discard all
thoughts of them that are to their dis-
credit.' (I felt that the colour was rising
in my cheeks; for the news I had just
heard had, I confess, set me thinking of
the wild doings and misdoings of my late
relative.) 'I don't know,' resumed my
father, after a pause, ' whether foolish
people have ever led you to believe that
your Uncle Tom's death would materially
benefit us; but if so, they were mistaken.
He has left two legitimate children, of
about your own age.'

'Two children!' exclaimed I with astonishment too great for chagrin (and in-

deed the idea of being my uncle's heir had never taken any hold upon my mind, though it had certainly been suggested to it by others). 'I did not know that he had been ever married.'

'Nor I, until to-day,' said my father quietly. 'But the fact is so, nevertheless. You have two cousins—twin boy and girl — whose acquaintance you will shortly make, for they are on their road hither already. They will live here, under this roof, until they come of age.'

Upon the whole, I was pleased to hear this news. I had long been too old for the society of the village boys: not pride, but the sense of incongruity, had put an end to such familiarity. We had nothing in common; and the idea of having a companion of my own age, and perhaps tastes, was very welcome. The subject, however, was not pursued by my father, with whom I at once commenced my studies as usual; but later in the day, I found Aunt Benita much more communicative. Uncle Tom, it seemed, had married soon after he reached India; but, for some reason or other, had concealed the fact from my father during all these years. He had probably, said my aunt, married greatly beneath him. The wife had long been dead, and yet neither of her decease nor existence had he written one line: that is, not by way of letter; but he had always carried about with him a certain document, addressed to my father, to be forwarded in case of his own death; and at last this had come to hand. Therein his two children were affectionately intrusted to his brother's care until they should attain the age of twenty-one, when the son (Cecil) was to come into his property, a very considerable fortune; and the daughter (Jane) would inherit four thousand pounds. If Cecil died childless, his fortune was to revert to myself (in order, said the document, that the house of Wray should be duly represented); but if Jane should die unmarried before him, her fortune was to go to her brother. Such, roughly stated, were the conditions of the will; in the mean time five hundred pounds a year was to be paid to my father for the maintenance of the orphans. Copies of the will, of my uncle's marriage certificate, and of the registration of the twin children's birth, were enclosed, and the London lawyer indicated to whose safe keeping the originals had been consigned. The children—if they could be called such, for they were nearly eighteen — were already on their way, as a letter informed us, written by a brother-officer of my uncle's, and announcing his decease. They might arrive, as Aunt Ben said, ' any day;' and she instantly set about her arrangements for their reception.

She seemed to me more shocked at my uncle's death than sorry for it, and I think she was deeply chagrined on my account to hear of the existence of these undreamed-

of relatives.   We had all known that Uncle
Tom was rich: every year a box of magnificent presents had arrived from India;
shawls for my aunt, not one of which she
had ever ventured to wear (where *could* she
have worn such shawls except at church?
and what chance would the discourses of
the Rev. Mr. Bourne have had against their
attraction, if she had?); precious manuscripts for my father, exquisitely illustrated, but, of course, wholly undecipher-
able; and inlaid yataghans, and bows and
arrows, for myself.   These wonderful gifts,
typical, in their uselessness and splendour,
of our empire in the East, were now, it
seemed, all that we should ever derive in
the way of advantage from Uncle Tom's
prosperity.   To do Aunt Ben justice, she
had no regrets upon her own account; but
I fancy she had entertained hopes that her
eccentric brother would one day return,
and make amends for his wayward youth
by rebuilding the fallen fortunes of our

house. 'At all events, I do think, my
dear, that he might have left your father
some special bequest, in consideration of —
But there, how should *you* know?'

In after years I came to the knowledge
of certain pecuniary sacrifices which had
been made upon my uncle's account by
his brother, to which I have no doubt this
remark of my aunt had reference. But my
father never once alluded to the matter,
nor, as I believe, ever gave it a passing
thought. The memory of his dead brother
was sacred with him. I shall never forget
the tone of sublime conviction in which,
when Aunt Ben hazarded the observation,
'I suppose there can be no doubt of the
genuineness of those documents which are
said to be in that London lawyer's hands?'
he replied, 'My dear, Uncle Tom has
said so.'

There was no lack of accommodation at
the Manor-house, so far as room was concerned, for half-a-dozen pair of twin cousins;

but it was evident that the arrival of my new-found relatives was to make a change in our way of living. There were many 'sympathising' callers as soon as the record of Uncle Tom's decease appeared in the papers, and my father made a point of returning each visit in person. 'You and I, Fred, gentle shepherds as we are, might shut ourselves up as we pleased,' he would say, smiling; 'but it is only right that your cousins should see the world, and it is my place to introduce them to it.'

Most of the good folks our neighbours were pleased at our being about to have these visitors; since the fact had already 'brought my father out,' as they termed it, as though he had been a *débutant;* for though a recluse in his habits, he made himself very agreeable when society was forced upon him : moreover, the event gave them something to talk about, which was a desideratum in Sandylandshire, as in one or two other country neighbourhoods with which I

afterwards became acquainted. Mr. Bourne
the elder, familiarly entitled by my father,
after Ben Jonson, 'the Alchemist' (he had
found the philosopher's stone in the sand-
cliff in the shape of a scythe-stone), was in
particular greatly elated by the news. His
imagination, which, if not powerful, did not
waste itself in mere luxuriant fancies, but
was concentrated on the one idea of money-
making, pictured my cousins as an Indian
prince and princess, and his heart went
forth to welcome them accordingly. 'The
idea, sir' (he used to call me 'sir' from the
age of ten)—'the idea of your Uncle Thomas
having made all that money : the last man
in the world, one would have said, to have
done it; but it does happen so sometimes—
sometimes.' And then he shook his hoary
head, and pressed his skinny lips, as though
he would have added, ' But not twice in
the same family, sir; mark that—*you* will
never make a shilling.' Perhaps he deemed

it possible that my cousins would wish to buy back the family estate, sand-cliff and all, and already scented a good stroke of business; or perhaps it was from mere greedful curiosity that the old man once ventured to inquire of my father whether these young people were so immensely rich as was rumoured.

'*They are Peru, sir*,' was the reply; '*great Solomon's Ophir*.'

'Gad, then,' said he, looking round on the somewhat dim and faded furniture of our room of state, 'you'll be put to it to entertain them fitly.—I mean,' added he quickly, made sensible by a flash from my father's eyes that his remark had not been the pink of courtesy. 'that you will have to spend a good deal of money in their reception.'

'You are right, my friend,' answered my father; ''tis fit we change

"All that is metal in this house to gold;
And early in the morning will I send

> To all the plumbers and the pewterers,
> To take their tin and lead up."

Rich! you say?

> " T' Hesperian Garden, Cadmus' story,
> Jove's Shower, the Boon of Midas, Argus' eyes,
> Boccace his Demogorgon, thousands more,
> Are abstract riddles of their wealth." '

' Thousands ?' exclaimed the old man, catching at the only word intelligible to him in this outburst. ' Why, they must have tens of thousands, and jewels too, I daresay!'

' Yes. indeed,' was my father's grave response; ' and, in particular, *the flower of the sun, the perfect ruby, which we call Elixir.*'

Out of this conversation a rumour went abroad that my cousins were bringing a sort of Koh-i-Noor with them, to be worn in the hat or the hair; so that the public curiosity to behold them was excited to the utmost. One solid pecuniary advantage old Mr. Bourne did glean out of the

event; for, hearing that my father had
dropped some hint of engaging a private
tutor for Cecil, he hastened down to the
Manor House to volunteer his son's services in that capacity. My father, although
surprised, was by no means displeased at
this officious zeal. The idea of a resident
tutor was not welcome; and, on the other
hand, it would not have entered into his
head to ask such a service of the pompous vicar ; for though the tithes that fell
to the share of that divine were small, he
was, as the son of the alchemist, held of
course as a most prosperous man. But
old Bourne dispelled this illusion very
quickly. 'My son has nothing, sir, but
what I choose to give him, except the
living, and even that I bought for him—
yes, sir, with my own hard-earned money.
What interest have I ever yet got for the
sums I spent upon his college education?
Not a shilling, sir ; not a shilling. Here
is an opportunity for making it bear a

little fruit, which I shall certainly not permit him to miss. Let him thole a bit, let him thole a bit, as I have done all my life.'

The idea of thus disposing of the services of a beneficed clergyman, of fifty years of age, just as though he had been arranging for a lad's apprenticeship, did not strike the old gentleman as being in any way unbecoming; and my father had the greatest difficulty—though he carefully avoided quotations from the Elizabethan poets—in making him understand that such an offer must needs emanate from the vicar himself. In the end, however, it did so, though in a. very different manner from that in which it had been made by proxy. The reverend gentleman was all carelessness and condescension— 'He had been given to understand that Mr. Wray had sounded his father with respect to his (the vicar's) undertaking the education of young Mr. Cecil; well, it was

true that he had some classical and mathe-
matical knowledge—perhaps as much as
most people who call themselves scholars;
but really, teaching was such drudgery;
and yet on the other hand, he would do
anything to oblige so respected a friend
and neighbour.' In the end, he concluded
the bargain to so great an advantage that
it would have done credit to the alchemist
himself, and might have sufficed of itself
(but for the existence of his daughter
Eleanor) to have established the theory of
the hereditary transmission of great qualities.

Nelly alone, of all our neighbours, regarded the coming of my cousins with dis-
favour. She foresaw in it an interruption
to our common studies and companionship,
and augured ill from it in all respects.
'You will be fast friends with Cecil,' said
she, 'and care for nothing but hunting
and sporting' (the stud at the Manor had
already been increased, and also the ar-

mory); 'and your cousin Jane will be exquisitely beautiful, and you will fall in love with one another, as cousins always do, and care no more for your poor little Nelly.'

I think this prophecy went far to mar its own fulfilment, at all events as far as its latter half was concerned; for the despair of the fair sibyl so moved me, that then and there I printed a kiss upon her cheek for the first time in my life (though there were a good many impressions taken afterwards), and swore an unalterable fidelity. Except Aunt Ben, which could scarcely be said to count as an experience of the operation, I had never kissed any one before; and the effect of that experiment was tremendous. I had already thought myself happy, but from henceforth I knew that I had been mistaken. The golden age of the world may have been the beginning of it, because man and woman were made grown up;

but the golden age of life does not commence in childhood. The songs of infancy are sweet, but there is no melody among them to be compared with that wordless music which the finger of first love evokes from the heart-strings.

Days and weeks passed by, more swiftly than I had ever known them to do so, and when our long-looked-for guests did come, I had almost forgotten that they were expected. Their arrival took place late in a July evening, just as our little household were preparing to retire to rest. The sound of wheels was heard far off in the avenue that led from the village. I saw Aunt Ben look up from her employment, which was darning stockings—for embroidery and fancy-work of all sorts, unless knitting can be so termed, she despised—and listen attentively.

'It is your cousins,' she whispered, for my father was deep in Webster (not the Dictionary), and did not like to be interrupted in his reading. But he had also heard the noise, and quietly read out the passage:

‘ I pray thee, look thou giv’st the little boy some syrup for his cold; and let the girl say her prayers ere she sleep;’

then closed the book, and went to the hall-door to receive the new comers.

There were no less than three carriages, for their luggage was extensive, and in the first, of course, were our guests. The twins were as like as it is possible for two human beings to be, and exceedingly plain, though there was something about them (to be mentioned presently) far more extraordinary in my eyes than their plain-ness. When they had been duly welcomed, Aunt Ben ushered Jane to her apartment, while I did the like office for Cousin Cecil. He thanked me graciously, but in somewhat guttural tones, which were the very echo of his sister’s; and I left him and returned to the drawing-room, whither

I found Aunt Ben had already repaired, and was talking alone with my father.

'Why, good gracious!' cried I, eloquent wih pent-up wonder, 'they are blackamoors!'

'Hush, for shame!' exclaimed my aunt. 'They are nothing of the sort; and if they are, it is not their fault.'

'But they *are*,' said I.—'Are they not?' appealing to my father.

He nodded gravely.

'"Black as the bird that in the silent night
Doth shake contagion from her sable wings."

The fact is—as perhaps we ought to have warned you, my boy—there is just a dash of the tar-brush in your cousins.'

I had indeed greatly exaggerated the swarthiness of their complexions, which was partly owing to their birth, but also to the effects of the Indian sun. They were not black, but black and tan, like terriers; still their colour could scarcely have astonished me more had it been magenta.

CHAPTER III.

NATURE, as I have said, had cast my twin cousins, with the exception of sex, in the same mould. They were as like as peas— dried peas, for their swarthiness had that withered and yellow look which so often belongs to the Asiatic. Their voices were so similar, that it was impossible for the ear alone to decide who spoke; and even their handwritings defied the eye to discern that of the brother from that of the sister. Their mutual affection was, moreover, such, that they loved one another as themselves, and this bond united them more closely than the natural ligament that bound together the Siamese twins. And yet, curiously

enough, we soon discovered that their dis-
positions were as opposite as the poles.
Cecil's nature was impulsive, generous, and
candid; that of his sister, secretive, proud,
and unconciliatory. Even Aunt Ben, with
whom (though she had her prejudices) no
human being had ever yet contrived to
quarrel, confessed that she could not 'get
on' with Cousin Jane. Kindness had no
power to impress her, and of course only
kindness was tried. At nineteen, she re-
sembled one of those cast-iron spinsters of
fifty, who regard even children with a stony
stare, and reserve their affections for a cat
or a dog, and when they die, leave all their
money to forward distant missionary en-
terprise. It was touching to observe the
efforts made by her brother to mitigate
(for her own sake, for she was never harsh
to *him*) the repulsive harshness of her manner, to bring warmth into her cold looks,
and when all was to no purpose, to excuse
her failings (as he tenderly imagined them)

to others; her health had suffered, he said,
from the change of climate; but we never
knew her to ail.

Though the faces of my cousins were
duplicates, the expression which their respective characters had evoked in each was
very different. In Jane's case, plainness
was so intensified by ill-humour, that she
was downright ugly; in Cecil's, plainness
was so mitigated by cheerfulness, that he
was almost comely. The intelligence of
both was very considerable; but here the
advantage lay on the other side. Jane
had taken every opportunity that India had
afforded — and there had been no stint
to Uncle Tom's provision for them in the
way of education—to improve her mind;
whereas the ignorance of Cecil was something stupendous. It is quite possible for
even a clever boy to emerge from a great
public school in England, after half-a-dozen
years' devotion to its so-called studies, with
the merest smattering of Greek and Latin,

and a total absence of information about
any other subject whether of use or interest; but Cecil had gone through his
Calcutta curriculum as a wild-duck dives
through the water and comes up again—
if not absolutely dry, yet scarcely damp.
Nothing, really nothing, remained about
him to evince that he had been to school
at all, unless I may except a passion for
private theatricals, an amusement to which,
it seems, the schoolboys of India are (or
were) much devoted. He had a good memory, was an excellent mimic, and had a
passion for what children call 'dressing-up,'
that in one of his years was rather ridiculous. His attachment to my father, with
whom, as indeed, with all of us, he soon
became a great favourite, led him to look
into that Elizabethan treasure-house, in
which the former so delighted; and though,
doubtless, he missed what was best, he
caught much of its humour, and repro-
duced it to admiration. I shall never for-

get him (all unconscious of plagiarism from Pistol), attired in full eastern costume, addressing our astonished cook in the sonorous words of Tamberlaine, and threatening the good soul with instant decapitation, as 'a pampered jade of Asia.' Singularly enough, considering his oriental extraction, he was far from slothful; very strong and active, and delighting in all out-door exercise. The use of a leaping-pole was, when he came to us, as unknown to him as the rest of the sciences; but, on the other hand, he took to it with avidity. My own high-flying expeditions had caused, as I have said, some little excitement in the neighbourhood; but that sank into insignificance compared with the wonder aroused by the feats of Cousin Cecil. Being in his novitiate, he was not, of course, so skilful a performer as myself; but his pluck was marvellous, and his conceptions, so to speak —his ideas of what was practicable—sublime. More audacious than the philosopher who only required a standing-point in order to move the world, he made light of even that mechanical difficulty. From a hedge-top, from a quaking bog, from a slippery house-roof, he would hurl himself through space with ambitious aim, and the most supreme indifference to the result.

It was not to be wondered at that the astonished villagers who beheld this flying portent of swarthy hue, associated him in their minds with the Prince of the Power of the Air, and called him 'our Gatcombe Devil.' Somehow or other, his sister got to hear of this, and it annoyed her extremely: she expressed her opinion that all such contumelious persons should be taken up and whipped; and when we laughed at the idea of such wholesale punishment, she was offended. As a matter of fact, Cecil was popular with everybody; his frankness and freedom from pride made their way to all hearts; nor, doubtless,

were the reckless feats, which won him
so disrespectful a misname, without their
charms. It was when he had been with us
a few months, that a circumstance occurred
in connection with this pastime—apparently
so innocent and unimportant — that was
fated to affect his future fortunes, and those
of all of us, in no small degree: on such
slight branches of the tree of life do great
fruits hang.

Our excursion on the day in question
had been extended beyond its usual limits,
to Wayford, an outlying hamlet of our village, through which the river Way ran;
and, indeed, it was the goodly breadth of
that stream which had attracted us thither.
Beside the Mississippi, or even the Thames,
its proportions would doubtless have seemed
small enough; but then we proposed to
fly over it. The autumn was far advanced,
and nature wore that pathetic look of
beauty which is peculiar to that epoch—
the same quiet grace of farewell that is

sometimes seen in the faces of the dying. The wind, even on the sand-cliff, did but whisper, and when we descended into the vale, was hushed. There was no sound in the moist air except that of the stream, that seemed to sorrow for the loss of summer, as it swept the banks no longer pranked with flowers. Its broadest part ran through an apple-orchard, the scanty leaves of which, like tempted innocence, were blushing before their fall. Between this orchard and the sand-cliff was a small cottage, the tenants of which were Ruth and Richard Waller—a sister and brother, who, having lost their parents in early youth, had contrived to keep the same home, and support themselves, though perhaps the youngest couple that ever adventured housekeeping. They were still young, not even being of age; but Richard dug for the scythe-stone, and that deadly toil had already affected his health. Ruth too performed that share of the work which usually fell to the lot of Gatcombe women.

We could hear across the stream, as we drew near, that chipping of the stone, which might have been likened to the graving of her own epitaph, so sure was it, if persisted in, in the end to prove her doom. At present, however, to judge by her looks, the nature of her toil had in no way injured her. Hearing our voices, she came to the cottage door, shading her eyes with her hand against the sun, and I thought I had never beheld a fairer picture. She was rather over the middle height, and of a most graceful figure; her complexion was as fair as though it had never been exposed to outdoor influences; and her fine brown hair shone in the sunlight like bright threads of gold. It is curious enough that though large eyes are preferred to small ones, there is a certain charm in eyes half-shut beyond any attraction they possess when open. True, there is a mechanical necessity in the former case to smile; but independently of that pleasant accompaniment, the glance shot through

half-closed lids is one of the deadliest wea-
pons in Beauty's armory.   In the present
instance it clove a heart to the centre.

'How are you, Rue?' cried I, for we
had known one another all our lives,
though, from Wayford being so far from
the Manor-house, we seldom met.

'Nicely, thank you, Master Fred.   I
hope the Squire and Miss Benita are in
good health.'

'How is your brother Richard?'

'Well, sir, he is but so-so.   He is working in the cliff, you know,' she added, as if
that was explanation enough of his not
being in rude health.

'And you, Rue, you are doing almost
as bad,' said I rebukefully.   'I wish you'd
let me bring you one of Aunt Benita's
masks; but there—I daresay you would be
too conceited to wear one.'

'Too beautiful rather, much too beautiful,' murmured Cecil's voice at my elbow;
his dark eyes gazing upon her with undis-

guised admiration, his dusky features aglow
with delight.

'My cousin Cecil says you are too beautiful,' cried I aloud; at which, with a rosy
blush, Rue vanished within doors.

'*Now all's dark,*' quoted Cecil from one
of my father's favourites, and with the full
meaning of the author in his deep tones
too.

He was not angry at my mischievous
repetition of his late remark; I think, on
the contrary, he was pleased that the girl
should have heard what he thought of her
marvellous charms.

'Well, let's have the light again,' said I,
laughing. 'Rue! Rue! do come out and
show us where there is firm footing: we
are going to leap the stream.'

She came out at once, and warned us
that the river was very deep just there.

'Pray, don't attempt it, Master Fred,
or the folks will say I helped to break
your neck. It is shallower and narrower

above yonder; and the banks are not so high.'

But it was the height of the bank at that particular spot which in reality made the project feasible. Between us and the cottage lay a miniature alpine ravine, which I had little doubt of being able to clear, if only the pole were long enough to reach the bottom of it. As for Cecil, he would have essayed to leap Niagara, even if Ruth Waller had not been waiting for him on the other side of the Falls.

I examined with care the ground which sloped down to the brink of the stream ; it was moist and slippery.

'We can't take any run at it,' said I doubtfully ; 'it must be a standing jump.'

'All right,' said Cecil carelessly, his eyes still rapt on the beautiful girl, who, on her part, was watching us with the utmost interest. 'I'm game.'

'I've no doubt of that,' said I, laughing ; 'but you'll be dead game, if you don't take

care what you are about; there isn't half a
foot of pole to spare, and if it breaks——
Upon my life, Cecil, I don't like it,' whispered I; 'one wants a fir-tree for such a
span as this.'

'Don't ye, don't ye try it, Master Fred,'
cried Rue appealingly, and perceiving my
hesitation. 'You talk of the rashness of
us poor people; but we work at our ill
trade for our bread, whereas it's sinful to
run such a risk as that for pleasure and—'

'If you are afraid, Fred, let *me* go,' said
Cecil quietly. 'Why, after all, it's only a
ducking at the worst.'

I knew very well that a ducking might
not be the worst of it; but my cousin's taunt
determined me at once to make the attempt; moreover, despite her entreaties,
there was a flush of colour in Ruth Waller's face which showed how deeply she was
interested in the performance of the feat,
and I did not like to disappoint the village
beauty. The words of the heralds in the

lists of Ashby occurred to me with ludicrous application to my position: 'Love of ladies, death of champions, splintering of lances! Stand forth, gallant knights; fair eyes look upon your deeds!' If the lance *should* splinter in the present case, it was not impossible that the death of the champion might ensue; but still I did stand forth, and looked as gallant as I could under the circumstances. First, then, I went through the somewhat unknightly performance of moistening the palms of my hands; then I grasped the top of the pole, the iron-shod end of which was already firmly placed in the stream; swayed backward and forward once or twice, drew in my breath, and finally launched myself into the air. It seemed to me that I took a long time to get across; the momentum was only just sufficient to throw the pole on the other side; and in the middle, I distinctly felt it 'hang;' the effect of which, had the retardation been maintained, would

have been to make me circle round the
pole, like a toy monkey, and then drop in
the river. But the good pole carried me
safe over, and almost into Ruth's arms.

'Eh, but you are a gey fine lipper, Master Fred!' said she with enthusiasm, as I
stood panting, and perhaps a little proud,
by her side.

It was now Cecil's turn to try his luck.
I had great doubts—though, of course, I
did not express them—of his safe arrival
at our side of the Way. He was not, as
I have already mentioned, so skilful in the
management of the pole as myself; while
I, for my part, had never made a more
difficult leap. It was not his habit, however, to lose much time in preparation, and
over he came like a rocket—that is, he
came about half-way over. When he got
so far, there was a splintering crash, which
made my blood curdle, for it told me that
the pole had given way, which is the great
danger of deep leaping. If he should come

down upon the broken piece, it might spit him like a lark, and this was just what he had done; and though, happily, he fell aslant upon it, the shock was so painful and violent, that it forced a sharp cry from his lips, which the next instant was stifled in the stream. Quick as a bird, Ruth flew down the steep steps that led from the cottage to the river's brink, and caught him by his clothes as the current swirled him by. Except that he was wetted to the skin, the ducking had done him no harm; but when he had struggled to his feet, we saw that his face was pale, and that he pressed his hand against his side, as though in pain.

'You are hurt?' said I anxiously.

'No, no; it's nothing,' said Cecil, who had been thanking Ruth in a faint voice. 'I'm a little bruised, that's all. I can't walk very well. I think I should be better if I could sit down a while;' and he looked towards the cottage.

'Do, pray, sir, come in,' said Ruth.

'But you'll catch your death in those wet clothes. Perhaps you wouldn't mind wearing Richard's Sunday suit, while I dry them before the fire?'

This offer was gratefully accepted; and I took Cecil at once up to Richard Waller's room, and helped him to change his attire. This was accomplished with great difficulty, for my cousin's breathing seemed much oppressed; and when he caught sight of himself in the little glass in corduroys and a red waistcoat, and would fain have burst out laughing, the attempt appeared to give him great pain.

'I tell you what, Cecil,' said I decisively, 'there's something wrong with your ribs. I'll leave you here under Ruth's care, and fetch Dr. Cherwell; and if he's not in, I'll at all events bring the pony-carriage from the Manor-house, for it's clear you can't walk home.'

I expected opposition to this plan, for Cecil hated to be made a fuss with—even

his sister's demonstrative solicitude about
his health, and the dangers of pole-leaping,
vexed him ; but, to my great relief, he
made none; so off I started on my errand,
leaving Ruth in charge of him. In those
days I could run like the deer; but it was
a long way to the doctor's, and when I
reached his house, he was away on his pro-
fessional round ; then, there was a mile or
two more to the Manor; and the groom
was not at the stables, so I had to put the
pony in the shafts myself, for I did not
wish to alarm the household, by letting
them know why I wanted the carriage. I
had accomplished my task with privacy,
and was driving at a canter down the
avenue, when, to my great confusion, I
met Cousin Jane. She stopped me at once,
and with a swift suspicious glance, inquired
whither I was going.

'I thought you were out with Cecil,'
said she. 'Where is he?'

I told her the plain truth. He had met

with an accident; there was nothing serious, but he was bruised, so that walking
gave him pain; and I was taking the pony-
trap to bring him home.

'You will bring him home dead,' cried
she vehemently, the fire glittering in her
dark eyes; 'and then you will get his
money, and be satisfied.'

'Jane!' cried I, in astonishment that
knew no bounds. 'What on earth do you
mean? You must be stark mad!'

'I was,' said she, controlling herself by
a great effort. 'Forgive me, Cousin Fred.
I am sane now. I am sure that you love
my brother, and would rather have him
grow up and be happy, than reap any
benefit at his expense. You have no selfish thoughts, as some have. Pray, forgive
me.'

She stepped lightly into the carriage,
and seating herself by my side, laid her
hand upon mine, and patted it, as though
it were the head of a child.

'I forgive you, of course, Jane,' said I, withdrawing from this caress; 'but how is it possible for me to forget such words? What selfish thoughts do you refer to, and who are those that entertain them? If you mean my father and Aunt Ben—and I know of no one else to whom you can possibly refer—I can answer for their never having harboured a base thought, even in their dreams. They would not speculate upon your brother's death for all the filthy dross that was ever picked up in India.'

How angry I was, and how I hated that yellow girl, who squatted beside me like a toad!

'You are shocked and ashamed of me, Cousin Fred,' said she penitently; 'and I deserve it.'

This I did not deny, but flicked the pony with the whip, and drove on rapidly through the village. When we had cleared it, and were cantering along the noiseless sand-road that ran round the foot of the cliff, Jane began to speak again, with great slowness and precision, like a secretary of some mercantile community making his statement in committee assembled.

'In my terror upon Cecil's account, Frederick, and in my anger too, for you know how I have always opposed this leaping, that has now turned out so ill, I said the first thing that came to my lips. It was never harboured in my thoughts at all; upon my word, it was not.'

'I think we had better drop the subject,' said I drily.

'As you please, Frederick,' was the humble reply; 'but do not imagine that I have not been punished.' She said this with such obvious mental pain, that I really pitied her.

We began to talk of Cecil's accident, and where I had left him, and the like; and she was all calmness and content.

'I am quite sure you did the best for him, poor fellow, that could be done. I daresay it will turn out that he has only a few bruises, which will have no other effect than to make him more cautious. Even a broken rib is not very serious.—My dear cousin, who is that horrible man?'

This ejaculation was caused by the appearance of poor Batty—as Bartholomew Cade, the harmless idiot of the village, was called. He had worked in his childhood in the sand-cliff; and a sudden fall of earth had deprived him of his senses, and left him only instincts, one of which was, unhappily, for drink. He had just arrived from the terrace on the road in front of us, by his usual method of descent, which was, to curve himself into a circle, and roll down like a wheel; and there he stood, shaking the sand from his head and limbs by a grotesque rotatory movement that would have addled the brains of any sane man. As we drew near, he held out a handful of copper and small silver coins, and laughed exultingly.

'How did you get all that money, Batty?' inquired I, as I drove slowly by, lest his weird antics and appearance should startle the pony.

'Selling props,' cried he — 'props, props!'

'I hope you didn't steal them, Batty?' said I gravely.

'No, no; I cut 'em with the bill-hook.'

As we drove on, I explained to Cousin Jane that this poor fellow earned his living by cutting out of the fir-wood the props for the sand-caves, which were bought of him for small sums by the workmen; and how, on one occasion, it had unfortunately struck him that his labour might be saved by taking the props out of a cave, and selling *them* — an idea which, but for the timely discovery of his theft, might have caused great catastrophes.

'I hope he was whipped,' said Cousin Jane tartly, with whom whipping was a panacea for all disorders, mental, moral, and physical.

'Nay,' said I. 'Batty is not responsible for his actions; but he has promised not to misbehave himself in the way of prop-stealing again, and he always keeps his word.'

Perhaps the notion of Batty's getting off so easily, outraged Cousin Jane's strict sense of propriety, but, at all events, for the rest of our drive she became more like her usual self. When we stopped at the end of the little lane which led to the cottage of the Wallers, and which was not practicable for wheels, she jumped out, and hurried on, leaving me to tie up the pony. When I followed, she had not entered the house, but was standing at the open door. I was about to ask her why she did not enter; but she shook her head, and held up her hand for silence. Her face was livid, her breath came in thick gasps, and her thin lips were parted

with a grin of rage. I looked over her
shoulder at the sight which had evoked
these unpleasant symptoms. In that apartment of a Gatcombe cottage which is
'kitchen, and parlour, and all,' sat, all
unconscious of our presence, a pair of
youthful rustics. The walls were but of
plaster, and defaced rather than orna-
mented by some highly-coloured daubs
of the story of the Prodigal, and of Ruth
amid the corn; on the mantelpiece, art
was again travestied in the person of an
infant Samuel, highly gilt, and with black
dots for eyes; on the shelves were a few
specimens of common delf; the floor was
carpetless; and from the roof depended
onions. And yet the human objects in this
frame redeemed its coarseness, and presented a fair picture—purest pastoral.
Pretty Rue, with head aside, and eyes
that feigned an interest in the burning
logs, was seated by the fire; and close to
her—so close that their chairs touched—

sat Cecil in the Sunday suit, with his hand pressed to his red waistcoat, like a love-sick Robin. What he was saying, I know not, but he was looking encyclopædias of affection.

Jane drew me on one side of the porch, and whispered hoarsely: 'Who is that woman?'

'Only Rue Waller. She pulled him out of the river, and lent him her brother's clothes. You see,' added I mischievously, 'Cecil is not so very much hurt by his accident — unless it induces heart-disease.' Here I gave a premonitory cough, which was followed by the hasty scraping of chairs within; and when we again presented ourselves at the doorway, the young people were on opposite sides of the fire-place. Rue was blushing like a peony; but Cecil's swarthy face did not change its hue (though it was prone to do so on slight occasion), nor move a muscle: in this respect it showed a striking contrast to its duplicate, for Jane had turned as nearly white as the nature of things permitted.

'I came here understanding that you were hurt, Cecil,' said she, with that distinctness of utterance so significant of pent-up rage. 'But it seems that you only wished to get rid of Frederick.'

'I might have been hurt,' returned Cecil quietly, 'had it not been for kind help and tendance.'

Jane laughed a little laugh, that was the concentration of contempt and scorn, and surveyed Ruth—to whom he had pointed, and who stood curtseying humbly, yet with great grace—from head to foot. 'Well,' resumed she, 'you have been tended long enough, I think. Is it not time to have done with your farce—to take off those ridiculous clothes, and come home?'

The duplicate faces became now alike in hue.

'I see nothing ridiculous in the clothes which have been so hospitably lent to me,' said Cecil sharply; 'but I see something very mean and base in jesting at honest people because they happen to be poor.'

There was a most embarrassing pause, during which the young hostess gazed on the fire, and brother and sister confronted one another with looks such as they had certainly never interchanged before.

Then 'Ruth,' said Cecil, with a tenderness in his tone that he seemed to exaggerate rather than to attempt to conceal, 'I am greatly obliged to you for your kindness. Your brother's clothes shall be returned to-night; and please to express to him my thanks for the use of them.' He held out his hand, which Rue shyly took, and, as he did so, turned round upon his sister defiantly.

'If you have not your purse with you, Cecil,' said she drily, 'I have mine. You should always remunerate for their trouble honest people who happen to be poor.'

'Indeed, miss,' said Ruth hurriedly— for Jane had already taken out three half-crowns and laid them on the table—'my brother would be very vexed to think that I took money for' —— The close of her sentence was lost in a passionate exclamation in Hindustanee; and Cecil snatched up the silver, and threw it, through the doorway, into the middle of the river, where the broken pole was still standing. What he said, I know not; but I am sure, from the expression which it evoked on his sister's face, that the Indian tongue is capable of conveying a strong invective; and after his retort, not a syllable of any language, European or Oriental, did Cousin Jane utter during our drive home.

CHAPTER IV.

THE pains which Cousin Jane took to set
herself right, after that unfortunate day's
proceedings, with both myself and her
brother, were great and unintermittent.
Directly she had made that speech suggestive of the advantage that would accrue
to us at Gatcombe if anything were to
happen to Cecil, I saw that she would
have given much to have recalled it: she
had looked, to use a popular and powerful
image, as though she could have bitten
her tongue out. Her apology and retracta-
tion had followed, as I have said, on the
instant; and yet she seemed painfully
aware that they had been insufficient.
If her insult had been directed to myself,

I could perhaps have forgiven her; but
the insinuation had been uttered, on her
own confession, with reference to my father
—the least self-seeking and mercenary of
men—and it had wounded me to the quick.
Her keen intelligence perceived this, and
her efforts to re-establish herself in my
good opinion were made through the very
channel in which she had made shipwreck
of herself. Her manner towards Uncle Fred
underwent a complete change; she discarded her sullen ways, and endeavoured
all she could to adapt herself to his genial
mood. She anticipated Aunt Ben in light-
ing his pipe and cutting his newspaper for
him after breakfast; and even took a part
in that long-established recreation of the
household, in which he took such unfeigned
pleasure, namely, our Dramatic Readings.
Hitherto she had icily declined to join
them, and had sat apart, engaged, with
pressed lips and knitted brow, over a certain intricate Chinese puzzle, and surrounded

with a faint atmosphere of sandal-wood (which I smell now), while Bobadil gave lessons in fence, or Mammon in making money. My father Bowdlerised his favourite plays (by no means a task of supererogation), to suit the drawing-room; and Aunt Ben and Eleanor from the rectory, who formed the female portion of our *dramatis personæ*, were hardly worked, and greatly needed Jane's assistance, thus tardily bestowed. There were no stage jealousies amongst us; and indeed Aunt Ben, for her part, would have gladly thrown up all her engagements in her niece's favour, had she been permitted to do so. The dear old soul once confided to me, that whenever her turn came to declaim or protest, to coquette or plead, she felt like some unhappy whist-player who has got the lead and doesn't want it. She would always have been 'fourth hand,' that is, as far from the leader as possible, and never have won a trick if she could have helped it. Her neighbours

on either hand were ever conscious of a
melancholy undertone in which she was accustomed to recite her part before it came
to her, just as a schoolboy in class occupies
himself with his own approaching task,
without taking an absorbing interest in the
classical renderings of his predecessors. She
had the advantage over him, indeed, of being able to calculate to a nicety, and of
not being liable to corporal punishment in
case of a fiasco; but she had her nervous
anxieties nevertheless; and often and often
would my father's grave remonstrant tones,
' Now, Benita, Benita!' remind her, like
some stroke of doom, that her turn was
come, and awaken her to the horrors of
her (dramatic) situation. Then would her
finger hurriedly retrace some fourteen lines
or so of heroic verse, and damp and palpitating, she would depict the woes of
Aspatia, and mildly reproach Evadne for
having robbed her of her Amintor. Happy
for her when Melancholy thus chanced to

mark her for her own — when she got a
plaintive part in the lot-drawing—and had
to recite such dirges as:

> ' Lay a garland on my hearse
>   Of the dismal yew ;'

for, indeed, they suited her feelings to a
nicety. Cousin Jane herself was not very
well adapted for the deliverance of pert
and lively sallies, but showed considerable
vigour in vituperation; in particular, she
once took my father's heart by storm in
playing Katherine to his Petruchio; on
which occasion, when we wished one another 'good-night,' she whispered in my
ear: 'I am so glad I pleased your father,
Fred.'

This touched me, and I repeated her
remark to Aunt Ben, who observed rather
drily, that Jane had seemed of late desir-
ous to please others beside my father.

'True,' said I; 'and much to her credit.'

To which my aunt made no reply. For
my part, I was certainly softened towards

Cousin Jane, and had by this time almost forgiven her monstrous insinuation with respect to Cecil. As for her brother, he had long been reconciled to her; though, if he had forgotten that scene in the Wallers' cottage, I am quite sure *she* had not. She showed her keen remembrance of it by never so much as alluding to the subject of his hurt (of which, indeed, he soon recovered), and by avoiding all inquiry into the mode in which he now passed his time. Instead, as formerly, of putting him through a cross-examination (borne with the utmost good-humour) on his return from each day's ramble, and of inveighing against the perils of pole-leaping, she merely hoped that he had enjoyed himself. She would still show her solicitude about him, indeed, by inquiring of *me;* but, as it happened, I could now tell her little of Cecil's proceedings. He was applying himself, it seemed, more assiduously than of yore to his studies with the rector, and would excuse himself from

my company on that ground. Thus it
happened that I fell back upon something
like the old mode of life that I had been
accustomed to before my cousin's arrival.
I had renewed opportunities of enjoying
Eleanor's society, and I took again 'long
stretches' across country by myself.

During these last, I now enjoyed a new
pleasure, namely, the composition of five-
act dramas of thrilling interest. My father's
tastes and talk, and our evening readings,
had at last brought about that condition
of mind which, had such circumstances not
been taken into the account, would have
been called a natural bent for the drama.
I wish carefully to avoid the imputation of
believing myself at any time to have been
a genius: the description of mental food
on which I had been nourished, and the
poetical atmosphere of my father's study,
were probably quite sufficient to account
for the existence of such a phenomenon as
a playwright of eighteen. At all events, it

did exist in my proper person; and once begotten, every incident in my experience tended to its development. My love for Nelly suggested passages of tenderest passion, which I would pour forth to her (very literally) *con amore*, and concerning which I would solicit her opinion without much fear of an unfavourable criticism; the society of Cecil was conducive to the same end, since, as I have said, the one cultivated talent he possessed was of a dramatic kind, while he had the advantage both of having seen plays acted, and of having taken part in them himself. Nothing would please him better, he said, as a profession in life than to be the Burbage to my Shakespeare; and I am sure he spoke from his heart, and had no conception that he was talking nonsense. Then there was a certain Lady Repton, from whom we had long been expecting a visit, who quite unconsciously played a considerable part in these shadow-plays of mine. She had been a great actress

—really a great one, in times when actors and actresses were thought of far more highly than nowadays; and a lord had carried her off the stage, and married her, to the grief of thousands. Lord Repton had been a college friend of my father's, and had promised 'some day' to come to Gatcombe, and introduce his wife to the only man in England who still appreciated the classical drama. I looked forward to this vague engagement with an eager expectation, such as a boy with the wild wish to be a sailor might have felt at whose father's house the immortal Nelson was a promised guest. Nor did I, in my inmost heart, despair of persuading her ladyship to reassume her profession, so far as to read a few of my own favourite declamations, in character, if not in costume.

In my walks upon the lonely sand-cliff, I apostrophised universal nature, and sent many a rabbit to his burrow palpitating with terror at my fervid words. On one

of these occasions, as, after a long ramble,
I was returning by the terrace, just above
Wayford, the rain began to fall so heavily
that, the shelter of the pines being insufficient, I made for the nearest sand-cave.
As I stood in the entrance of it as in a
porch, and watched the landscape darken-
ing and dwindling in the downpour, I heard
a noise from the interior—the trundling of
a barrow: the proprietor, whom I knew to
be Richard Waller, was doubtless at his
work within; and I stepped out of the narrow passage and stood aside, in order to
give him egress. A barrowful of the rough
scythe-stone in truth it was; but the person
who wheeled it turned out, to my extreme
astonishment, to be my cousin Cecil. My
surprise, however, was surpassed by his
confusion. He stood speechless, holding
the handles of the barrow very tightly, as
amateurs at such labour do, replying to my
wondering looks by an uneasy laugh.

'Why, what on earth are you about,

Cecil?' asked I. 'I thought you were going to be busy with your books all the
afternoon.'

'So I was to have been,' returned he;
'but Mr. Bourne was called away to chris-
ten a sick child; and I thought I'd come
on here, and help poor Waller. His breath
is getting very short, you know; and I
wanted a little exercise, and—and here I
am.'

He was certainly there, though it was
somewhat difficult to recognise him. His
hair and clothes were covered with sand;
his face was damp, as I supposed with toil,
and wore the pinched and anxious look
that was to be observed in those who pursued his present occupation for a livelihood.

'I don't think your sister would like
to hear you amused yourself in this way,
Cecil,' said I gravely, for I was really
alarmed at his appearance. 'It's far worse
than pole-leaping, my good fellow.'

'I shall amuse myself as I please,' returned Cecil haughtily, 'without consulting my sister or anybody else.'

'Nay, Cecil,' remonstrated I, 'you should know me better than to suppose me capable of dictation; but this work, believe me, is very unhealthy; and if you come here often' (here he dropped his eyes, and bit his lips), 'it will most certainly injure you in the end. It's no use your being angry with me, as I see you are. I don't want you to come to harm at Gatcombe, although I *am* your heir-presumptive, cousin.'

I spoke this with some bitterness, instigated by the remembrance of his sister's base suggestion, and the next instant regretted my irritation. I expected him to exhibit extreme displeasure, whereas he only replied humbly,

'I am sure, Fred, you wish me nothing but good. I daresay what you have said is very true. I won't help Waller in this way any more. Let us go home.'

'Nay,' said I, ' let us wait till the storm is over.'

I saw that my cousin was very impatient to be gone, but I was greatly averse to leave shelter and be wetted through to the skin, when five minutes' waiting would prevent it. Perhaps I was a little piqued, too, at Cecil's having preferred Richard Waller's company to mine, when he found himself freed from his studies (for he knew the direction my walk had taken, and might have met me if he chose), and was consequently disinclined to be conciliatory. The clouds began to disperse, and the sun had already tinged the distant fields, when suddenly the sound of some one singing within the cave, and evidently approaching us, delayed my footsteps on the very point of departure.

'I should have thought Richard Waller had no breath to spare for singing,' whispered I to Cecil.

'That's not Richard,' said he; and though

his tone was careless, I saw him colour deeply; 'it's Rue;' and at that moment Ruth (or Rue, as the neighbours called her) appeared at the cave-mouth, having in her apron a number of rough scythe-stones, which she dropped upon the ground on seeing me, without an effort to reclaim them.

'Lor, there!' cried she, finding her voice much more readily than Cecil had done in *his* first moments of embarrassment, 'you gave me quite a start, Master Fred! Who'd ever have thought of seeing *you?* Richard and I were only saying the other day, how long it was since we had seen aught of you at Wayford.'

She ran on, in a manner quite unusual with her, and never once, I noticed, looking towards my cousin, who, under cover of this sustained volley of words, began to collect his scattered powers, and presently to add his voice to hers. As for me, I held my tongue, my mind not suggesting

any original remark appropriate to the occasion, nor even recalling one out of the
wide range of my dramatic reading, rich
as it was in 'surprises' and 'situations.' If
Ruth Waller had dropped from the clouds,
instead of emerging from the earth, I could
scarcely have been more taken aback by
her appearance; not, indeed, that there
was anything wonderful in her being in
her brother's 'pit'—for so the caves were
called, though they were horizontal—but
only in her being there in Cecil's company.

'Richard is a good worker, you see,
though so scant of breath,' stammered my
cousin; 'and he can supply more than a
barrowful of scythe-stones at a time; so
Ruth and I both help to carry them out.'

'I understand,' said I drily; for indeed
so much of the matter was clear enough.

'Perhaps Master Fred would like to
see Richard,' suggested Ruth to Cecil.

Her coolness staggered me, but had a

contrary effect to that which it was designed to have; the familiarity of her address at once suggested to me that this could not have been the first time by many that my cousin and she had met since the day of his accident at Wayford. Moreover, her hint of Richard's presence in the pit had a savour of prudery about it, which, under the circumstances, did not impress me favourably with the fair speaker. That her brother *was* actually in the cave, I had no doubt, since, in the silence that followed her last remark, I could hear the strokes of his pickaxe as they grated against the stone, or fell muffled on the damp and yielding sand.

'The rain is over for the present,' said I quietly; 'we had better be off at once before there's another storm, Cecil.' And without waiting for his reply, I started at my usual pace for home.

My cousin remained behind for a few moments, as I knew he would, and presently overtook me. We walked on without speaking for some time, then he laid his hand upon my shoulder, and we both stood still.

'You are not pleased with me and Ruth, I fear,' said he.

'I am not my cousin's keeper,' replied I coldly; 'but if you ask me whether your behaviour seems to me judicious, I must honestly tell you, I do not think it is.'

'Judicious?' reiterated he, with scornful vehemence. 'What, in heaven's name, would you have me do, Fred? I love this girl with all my heart and soul; nothing shall part me from her — nothing, *nothing!* I am only happy when I am with her. What other excuse can I frame for being in her company than that of helping her brother in the pit? You, who pride yourself on your ingenuity, tell me *that.*'

Disturbed as I was by this confession, I could scarcely help smiling at his asking me to frame an excuse for the very interviews which were the cause of my uneasiness.

'My dear Cecil,' said I, 'the whole affair is bad, believe me, and will be worse in the end than at the beginning.'

'What do you mean by that?' inquired he, almost with ferocity. 'Do you suppose I mean Ruth harm? Do you take me for a blackguard?'

'No, Cecil, I don't; if I did, I should go straight to my father, and tell him precisely what has happened. If you were otherwise than the noble-hearted, affectionate fellow I know you to be, I should have seen Richard just now, and told him to his face that he was helping to bring his own sister to shame. It is useless to be angry with me, Cecil; such would, I assert, without doubt be the result in nine cases out of ten. In yours, the best that can possibly come of such a courtship is still disappointment and disgrace.'

'Why disgrace?' asked my cousin sharply.

'Because it would be disgraceful in one of your position to marry one in hers.'

It may be objected that for a young gentleman whose studies were dramatic, my judgment was somewhat too practical and commonplace. But there were many reasons that compelled this apparent inconsistency. In the first place, I foresaw the distress that such an attachment must needs cause my father, as my cousin's host and guardian; in the second, although I had had small experience of the world, the nature of my reading had developed a perception of the character of others which was rarely at fault; and my late interview with Ruth had impressed me with the conviction that the girl was crafty, if not designing.

As for the whole tone of the discussion between my cousin and myself, I am quite aware that it was something

quite different from what it would have
been had we had the advantage of a pub-
lic-school education. My father's teaching
had fixed within me a respect for women,
which Beaumont and Fletcher had not
destroyed. In this respect, he would even
have been deemed Quixotic; for his very
definition of cowardice was about the
same which the man of honour and the
world applies to gallantry. As soon as
I was old enough to understand him, he
had taken pains to convince me that in-
feriority of station in a woman, considering
her natural tendency to idolise mere rank,
ought to be as much her safeguard with
generous hearts as are, in other matters,
the innocence of childhood or the feeble-
ness of age; and I had at least imbibed
so much of his lessons as disinclined me
for that ribald talk and thought of women so common among those who have
acquired, with the rudiments of the ancient
classics, the tone of fashionable schools.

As for Cecil, he was incapable of a deliberate baseness; and by nature so frank, that it was impossible he could be deceiving me as to his real intention. I did not, therefore, fear for Ruth as I did for him. Her marvellous beauty was cause enough for any man's falling in love with her; whereas I opined that Rue Waller was not the girl to forget the plain features and dusky hue of my cousin Cecil in her appreciation of the qualities of his heart. That he did not forget them himself was evident from his reply to my observation, that marriage with one in Ruth's position would be disgraceful.

'Position?' echoed he. 'Do you sup. pose, then, that I don't know what is *my* position as compared with yours, or, if your kindness mislikes so personal a comparison, compared with that of your father? I am—God help me!—but an ignorant half-caste; only tolerated—I will not say by you or yours, but by the world at large—on account of my wealth. Without my riches, for what should I be valued—I had almost said, cousin, by whom?' He dropped his voice, and spoke these last words with a tender pathos that went to my heart.

'Cecil,' said I, 'it pains me to hear you speak in this manner; and yet what you have said emboldens me to use an argument which otherwise I should have shrunk from. If, indeed, you be such as you describe (though your face is comely enough in my eyes, and the blood that moves in your veins seems that of a brother), and if it be your wealth alone that is likely to attract strangers towards you, what is it, think you, that has attracted this young girl, whose poverty must, by contrast, have made your riches seem to her to be ten times as great as they really are?'

'You are right,' returned Cecil quietly. 'Ruth loves me not, except for the wealth that I shall bring her. But I love her for herself; and it is enough for me that she does not loathe me.'

I looked at him with wonder, in which, perhaps, some contempt involuntarily mingled.

'Ah! you fancy you have loved,' said he, in low grave tones, with an affectionate smile; 'but you have never really done so, Fred; or rather, I should say. it is not possible that your love and mine should be of the same sort. You and Eleanor have each something to give, something to exchange; but, to the woman whom I would fain persuade to love me, I have nothing to give — nothing to barter for her love; so, you see, Fred, *I must buy it.*'

Never shall I forget the air of indescribable wretchedness with which he uttered those words.

'I have never deceived myself in this matter,' continued he, 'and much less

Ruth. To affect to help her brother at his work in yonder pit is, indeed, a feeble pretext of sympathy, which imposes upon neither of us; but I can't give him money, Fred. When she asks me for it—which, perhaps, she will do some day—then it will be time enough to give him money, and so to buy her.'

If Cecil's face was plain, it was at least freighted with an emotion more tender and pitiful than I had ever seen expressed in human features. And he was going to waste all that wealth of love upon a woman whose perceptions would probably never detect its existence, and who would —to judge her even by his own estimate —be doubtless prepared to exchange for it a few hundreds of pounds! The thought of a compromise had, indeed, at first occurred to me; but no one who now beheld Cecil's face, and heard his tones, could have entertained it for a moment. Whatever *she* might have taken, nothing

but herself, I felt sure, would have contented *him*.

'And how is all this to end, Cecil?'
asked I; 'for every dream must have some
end.'

He took no notice of the tone of incredulity, which, I confess, was affected
rather than real; for my cousin's nature
I knew to be full as resolute as it was impulsive.

'The end is, Fred, that I shall marry her.'

'Nay,' said I; 'that will be but the
beginning of the end—the first step in a
life of wretchedness.'

'We cannot foretell the future, cousin,'
answered he quietly; 'but, unless something happens, I shall marry Ruth when
I come of age.'

'Unless what happens?' inquired I,
pleased to hear that he was in no passionate haste, and in good hope that some
loophole of escape for him would present
itself in the intervening years.

'Unless your father comes to hear of
it,' said he, 'in which case I shall marry
her at once—at all hazards.'

There was nothing to prevent him.
Nor was my father the man, even if he
had the power, to adopt any stringent
measures in such a case. 'It will be a
sad blow for your sister Jane,' said I, ex-
pressing a reflection rather than advancing
a new argument.

For the first time, a shadow of irre-
solution seemed to flit across his face;
but it passed away immediately, leaving it
calm and determined as before. 'If my
sister gets to know of it,' said he, 'that
would have the same effect of precipitat-
ing matters.' Here he hesitated. 'But
I tell you frankly, Fred, that I wish her
not to know. It would not shake my
purpose — nothing can, nor shall. But
might I ask you, being more near to me
as friend than kinsman, not to tell her, not
to tell any one about Ruth?'

What could I do but promise? What was the use of telling when the news would only hasten on his rash resolve to its fulfilment? So I said: 'Your secret, Cecil, is safe with me. I would that I could wish you joy of it.'

'You do not wish me ill, I know,' said he, with his winning smile.

I shook my head. Indeed, I did not wish him ill, but I knew that ill awaited him. I think he knew it too; but neither he nor I could have imagined, nor even have dreamed, save in some weird, horrid nightmare, the shape that ill was doomed to take.

CHAPTER V.

A SPY-GLASS.

THE secret that Cecil had confided to me remained of course undivulged, nor did we even speak of it to one another. It was useless to discuss a subject whereon there was not only no possibility of our agreement, but in which my cousin had allowed that all the sense and reason were on my side, the infatuation and resolve on his. I felt that the plot was thickening, and for some time awaited the catastrophe with anxiety and trepidation : to borrow a metaphor from my favourite pursuit, I looked every day for 'a strong situation,' 'a scene' in which my father, Jane, and Cecil would prove the principal characters, and I my-

self be stigmatised as an accessory before
the fact; but as weeks and months passed
by without sign, I grew more tranquil; just
as one who, on board a powder-ship, has
seen his friends smoking their pipes for
years without an explosion, begins to think
there can be no such very great danger in
the practice after all. It was true that
Cecil, though showing even a warmer affection for me than heretofore, was more seldom my companion out of doors than ever,
and I could not but conclude that he was
passing his time in Ruth's society; but engaged myself in an equally pleasant way
with Nelly, I either grew insensibly more
tolerant, or became willingly blind to consequences in his case, as I did in my own.
For, regarded by unimpassioned eyes, my
courtship of Eleanor was almost as injudicious as Cecil's devotion to Ruth. I had no
fortune of my own whatever, and even on
my father's death would only succeed to a
very moderate estate; while Nelly was en-

tirely dependent on her grandfather, whose
favourite boast — and one which he was
wont to brandish in his son the rector's
face, to the great irritation of that learned
man—was, that he could leave every far-
thing of his money to whom he chose—' Ay,
sir, though it were to the County Lunatic
Asylum.'

Sometimes I fancied, from Jane's manner, that she suspected something amiss in
her brother's proceedings; but, much to
my satisfaction, she had long since ceased
to inquire concerning them of me. My
father was the very last man to whom an
idea of anything of the sort would suggest
itself; his confidence in the good conduct of
all beneath his roof being supreme. My
aunt concerned herself solely with the affairs of the house and of the village; and
besides, as maiden aunts are apt to do, she
considered Cecil and myself as boys; young
gentlemen of too tender years to be suspected of a serious passion.

Thus matters stood, when a letter from the north apprised us one morning that Lord and Lady Repton were at last about to pay their promised visit. My father handed it to me with a smile. 'There's a message for you in it, Fred, from the great tragedienne;' and I took it with trembling fingers. It was a wordy and pompous epistle (though the writer evidently intended to be cordial), and gave me no high opinion of his lordship's talents; but the contents of the postscript made my heart beat. 'Lady Repton bids me say that, in coming to Gatcombe, she looks forward not only to the pleasure of making the acquaintance of my old friend, but of his son, young Shakespeare.' I was mercilessly roasted about that message; my father called me 'the marvellous boy;' and Cecil sketched out with great humour a newspaper paragraph, headed *Elopement in High Life from Gatcombe Manor.* But I believe they both sympathised with my excitement.

Once again my cousin reperused with me my little stock of original dramas, all of which had been indebted to him for some stroke of fancy, if not for whole speeches, and even scenes, in the old days when we had 'Beaumont and Fletchered' it together; and out of them we chose what we judged to be the best to lay before this coming Siddons. I pictured to myself a heroine of imposing port, who would talk blank verse, and, when silent, look unutterable things. I dreamed of her as the Tragic Muse, investing my brows with a crown of amaranth. In my walks with Eleanor herself, I grew taciturn and meditative, and when asked reproachfully what I was thinking of, would reply with audacious frankness, 'Of Lady Repton.'

At last the morning of the day of her arrival dawned. I had not the courage to go and meet her on the road (I say *her*, because his lordship did not excite within me a spark of interest; we had a fair sprinkling of lords in Sandylandshire, with most of whom I had some acquaintance, and the Wrays of Gatcombe held up their own heads too high to bow before mere title). I walked out upon the brow of the moorland, and, with a glass, swept the road from the railway station, until my eyes hit upon her approaching carriage. I knew it by its four post - horses, without which, as my father told me, my Lord Repton never travelled ; and it was perhaps from the knowledge of that circumstance, combined with the laboured style of his letter, that I had come to the conclusion that he was a pompous and pedantic old fellow. The road wound beneath me, here a ribbon, there a thread, for miles; and there was more than an hour to spare from the moment I first caught sight of them to that when it would be necessary to turn homewards, in order to welcome their arrival. In the mean while, I sat down on the moor, and watched their approach, or surveyed the spreading landscape, clad in the pale green of spring. While thus engaged, and my gaze happening to be directed towards Wayford, I noticed a female figure emerge from the fir-wood, and come rapidly towards me across the moor. At first, merely because I associated her with the locality from which she seemed to come, I thought it was Ruth Waller; but the figure was taller than Ruth, and, as I soon remarked, attired far better than that rustic beauty had ever been. She wore a veil, which prevented me for some time from recognising her; but at last, to my extreme astonishment, I discovered that it was Cousin Jane. I was surprised; for Jane was a girl who hated walking, not from laziness, for she was by no means wanting in energy, but because it was such a vulgar thing to do. The commonest persons walked, and she wished it to be well understood that she was not a common person. If she could have been carried in a palanquin by obsequious bear-

ers, with a relay of those human beasts of
burden running behind her, she would, I
think, have taken a good deal of outdoor
exercise; but as it was, she restricted her
walks to the grounds about the house; she
never accompanied my aunt in her little
expeditions into the village, except to pay
a state visit, once a month or so, at the
Rectory; and deemed even taking a seat
in the pony-carriage a condescension: yet
here she was, miles away from home, alone,
and on Shanks his mare! On what errand
could she have gone to that fir-wood? in
which lay no other attraction than that
which drew her brother thither, I knew
not how often—but it might be five days
out of seven. Was it possible that the same
magnet, though from a very different cause,
had likewise attracted her? I trembled for
poor Cecil, and felt, I confess, not a little
uncomfortable upon my own account, as
the accomplice, or at least the confidant, of
his misdemeanours. If I was correct in

my suspicions, there would without doubt be a domestic tornado of the first magnitude.

She came on at rapid speed, like a thunder - storm (as I imaged her) against the wind; and so busily was she engaged with her own thoughts, that she would have passed me without notice, had I not sprung up and addressed her—not that I was anxious to be the first to meet her wrath, but because, if my fears were well grounded, I wished to prevent her going straight to my father, and troubling him with such grievous news just at the moment of our guests' arrival. That something had agitated Jane most deeply, I could see, though she still kept her veil down, and even held it with her hand, as though she was aware that her features told a tale that she would have concealed; but her voice was quiet and composed as she expressed her surprise at seeing me.

'Why, I thought you would have been

miles away, Fred, on the road to meet your play-actress!'

This remark was injudicious, for I at once concluded that she had counted upon my absence in that direction to keep her own expedition secret. She doubtless spoke on the impulse of the moment, for even her contemptuous mode of referring to Lady Repton showed naturalness and lack of design.

'Nay,' said I, 'it is I that should be astonished. I had no idea that your dainty limbs could have carried you so far. May I ask what was the inducement?'

'I had a headache,' she replied, 'and your Aunt Ben recommended me to try the moorland air.'

'Well, I hope it has done you good. cousin?'

'Yes,' said she, with a curious gravity in her tone; 'it has: it seems to have cleared my brain.'

'You should have tried the fir-woods,'

observed I carelessly; 'Dr. Cherwell says that their pungent scent is worth all the aromatic salts in the world.'

'I did try them,' returned she : 'I went into the pine copse above Wayford.'

'Perhaps you would not be quite so frank, cousin,' thought I, 'if you had not observed that I carry a telescope.' If she had really discovered anything, it was plain that she was not going to disclose it ; and if, on the other hand, she had nothing to disclose, there was no harm in my continuing my cross-examination.

'Did Aunt Ben recommend you to wear a veil ?' inquired I. 'I should have thought that all the air you could get on such a day as this would not have been too much.'

'I am not so hardy a plant as you, Fred,' she rejoined; 'but, as you say, it is warm now.—There, does *that* please you ?' and she threw up her veil with a forced laugh.

'Of course it pleases me,' said I gallantly; though, as a matter of fact, I had
never seen Cousin Jane look so uncomely.
Her face had the same livid look which I
had seen on it but once before (when she
had stood in the porch of Richard Waller's
cottage), and her lower lip was bitten
through and bleeding. As thus she smiled
upon me, and showed her glistening teeth,
the idea of a terrier, that had been fight-
ing with rats, occurred to me involuntarily;
and rather to escape from such a spectacle
than with any other motive, I offered her
the use of my telescope.

'You have keen eyes, Cousin Jane, and
if you can really discover the sea from this
spot, as my father contends we can, this is
the very day for the experiment.'

She thanked me, and taking the instrument, turned it in the desired direction,
which was over Wayford Wood. Her hand
did not 'wobble' with the weight of the
glass, as is the case with most women when

they take an observation with that instrument, but was as steady as a rock.

'You don't see it, Jane, do you?' said I, after a little.

'No; but I should like to do so. I won't give it up yet.'

There was something so peculiar, so curt and decisive, as though I had threatened to take the glass from her by force, in the tone of her last words, that it drew my own gaze from the carriage of our guests, which was now plainly to be seen nearing the village, and transferred it to herself. Then I noticed that the telescope was depressed, so as no longer to command the horizon, but was fixed upon the terrace beneath Wayford Wood.

'I think I see it now,' said she hoarsely; 'just a thin blue line—'

'But you are looking too much inland, Jane—if you'll allow *me;*' and I offered to take the glass.

In an instant she had dropped it fifty

or sixty feet upon the terrace below, where it, of course, was smashed to atoms.

'Dear, dear! how very stupid of me, Fred!' said she; 'it was all my own clumsiness. O, I *am* so sorry.'

It was certainly through her fault that the thing had happened; but I was by no means sure that clumsiness had anything to do with it. She seemed to me to have dropped it with malice prepense.

'Pray, forgive me, Fred,' continued she. 'The first day I go to Monkton, I will get you another, twice as good; that is'—for I suppose my countenance showed that I rather resented that form of indemnity— 'if you wouldn't be offended.'

'The ground is soft, and perhaps there is no great harm done after all,' said I; and in two or three bounds, after the Gatcombe fashion, I had descended the steep cliff and reached the terrace. I was not sorry that Jane could not follow me. I was angry with her, not so much for dropping the

glass, as for supposing that mere money
could supply a substitute for what she
knew I valued as my father's gift. That
was so like her. She did not even wait
to see whether it was destroyed; for when
I had picked up the fragments and looked
towards the spot where she had stood, she
was no longer there. She had doubtless
hastened home. At that moment I heard
the rumble of the Reptons' carriage in the
village street, and turned to follow her ex-
ample; but, as I did so, caught sight of
Cecil coming along the terrace from Wayford. I knew that black speck in the distance to be him from the rapidity of its
movement; for, when alone, my cousin always ran like Man Friday, or as though
he bore the Fiery Cross—it was a vent for
the superfluous energy of his nature. I
had not to wait long before he came up
with me, wide-eyed and panting; his dark
cheeks warmed with colour, and his whole
face so bright and joyous, that I had scarce

need to ask, ' Have you seen Ruth to-day,
Cecil?' It was the first time I had spoken
of her for months; indeed, the only time
since our one serious talk together upon
the subject, and I felt some degree of embarrassment in alluding to her. But Cecil
answered, with all possible simplicity: ' Yes,
Fred; I have but just parted from her.'

' On the terrace,' said I, ' or in the
wood?'

' It was just at the edge of the fir-
wood.'

' So I thought,' replied I gravely. 'To
that parting—a very tender one, no doubt
—your sister was a witness. It is no great
consequence, however,' added I, ' for I believe her suspicions had no need of such
confirmation. I am much mistaken if she
has not been watching you all the afternoon.' Then I told him how I had seen
Jane come veiled out of the fir-grove, where
Richard Waller worked; how angry she had
looked behind that veil; and how she had

dropped the telescope, to prevent, as I believed, my being a witness as well as herself to his tender adieus. 'That you are discovered, Cecil,' said I in conclusion, 'I feel quite convinced.'

'No doubt, no doubt,' said he, but in an irresolute tone, and looking yearningly towards Wayford, as though, since matters had reached this pass, he had half a mind to return *thither*, instead of to Gatcombe· 'I think, however, Jane will keep the matter secret, Fred; otherwise, why should she not have disclosed it to yourself?'

'Perhaps she means to appeal to you in private,' suggested I.

Cecil shook his head, still wearing that troubled air. If he had been capable of fear, which I knew he was not, I should have said he was afraid of his sister; but, at all events, it was evident that the idea of her displeasure was a source of the greatest disquietude to him. He walked home by my side, dejected and silent; and

his despondency seemed to communicate itself to me.　I could not shake off a sense
of some impending evil, so strong and so
engrossing, that even the long-looked-for
delight of meeting Lady Repton was already robbed of half its relish.

CHAPTER VI.

LADY REPTON'S RIDDLE.

By the time we got home, our guests had arrived, and Lady Repton had retired to her room to dress for dinner. His lordship, who was conversing with my father in the drawing-room, received Cecil and myself with affability and a couple of stretched-out fingers, sparkling with rings. His knuckles were so swollen with the gout, that it was as great a wonder how the rings got there as how apples are found in dumplings. He would certainly never get them off again in this life; and I could not help wondering within myself whether, when he was dead, his executors (or on whomsoever the duty might devolve) would cut off his fingers, or commit all those

precious stones to the grave. (What *is*
generally done, by the bye, in such painful circumstances?) His complexion was
very beautiful, and gave him an appearance of youth, which was renewed (like
the eagle's) every morning. His hair and
moustaches were black and silky. His teeth
were very white and fine; and yet one's
first idea upon seeing him (which was also
a permanent one) was, 'What a very old
gentleman this is!'

If you referred to the *Peerage*, however,
you would find that John Lord Repton
was by no means so very old for a peer
of the realm—a class which emulates for
longevity that of life-annuitants and incum-
bents of college livings. He was a ruin—
but comparatively a modern one—of the
renaissance style. His air and manner were
not only artificial; they did not belong to
real life at all. Congreve or Wycherley
might have created him. When he patted
his snuff-box, and took a pinch, raising his

jetty eyebrows, one naturally expected him to ejaculate, 'Stap my vitals!' In place of that appropriate remark, he would cry, 'Good gad!' in a sharp, shrill voice, and hand the box to the nearest person, though it were Aunt Ben or Jane. He prided himself on many things: his rank, his wife, his castle in Yorkshire, and his filbert nails; but, above all, upon his taste in literature. Upon this point my father would as soon have thought of giving in to him, or to any man, as of kissing the pope's toe; and very stubborn arguments they were wont to have together, which always ended by Lord Repton saying, 'You may be right, sir—you *may* be; but, gad! I used to have some little reputation as a critic too.' Indeed, from the constant use of that expression, he had been well known in London in old days as Reputation Repton. He took a great fancy to Cecil from the first, and nicknamed him (to his great indignation) Tippoo, after Tippoo Sahib; the

plunder of whose treasury had, as I afterwards learned, proved the foundation of
the Repton fortunes. His lordship's father
had been in high command in India, and
one of his uncles had been among those
brave English captives who, refusing to
serve the tyrant's guns against their fellow-
countrymen, had been decapitated by his
order. To hear the old gentleman narrate
the story was a great treat; the chivalrous
incidents of the affair were comparatively
disregarded, but his description of the 'loot'
which ensued after the assault of the British was very vivid and picturesque. 'I
had it from my noble father's own lips,
sir. . . . There were no less than three
thousand horses, one hundred elephants,
and two hundred camels, in that great po-
tentate's private stud; and, begad! six hundred women;' at which point in the nar-
ration he would wag his wicked old head
so very appreciatingly, that it was a marvel
he did not wag his wig off.

If his lordship was not very good-natured, he was very courtly, and fell at once to praising the old Manor-house in a way that was most grateful to my father. 'Now, I like this,' he would say; 'there are no gimcracks; everything is solid and serviceable. We have no such oak panelling as this in Yorkshire; these thick walls and deep bay windows are just to my taste. The garish lightness of your modern houses is my detestation: all here is shadow and calm, and breathes of ancestry; just as the layers of the cedar, with their depths of shade, betoken the revolving years. Do you see the image?—Take a pinch—take a pinch, young sir;' which, in my uncalculating courtesy, I did, and nearly sneezed my head off.

'That's a bad sign,' said his lordship gravely. 'A man of birth should take to snuff as naturally as a duck to water. If I had not known your sainted mother, sir, I should entertain suspicions of your not being a Wray of Gatcombe. Gad ! I remember the days when your father here took bushels of it.'

As I was well aware that my father had never taken a pinch of snuff in his life, this latter sarcasm at least fell pointless. Lord Repton's memory was not so good as it had been ; and since to repair it was impossible, he had hit upon the ingenious device of constructing a past out of his imagination, and quoting its events as though they had in reality occurred. My father never contradicted him on such points—even when he himself was introduced upon the stage, as in the present instance—but contented himself with a smile of incredulity equal to a folio. To do his lordship justice, this habit had become so natural with him, that he was far more persuaded that he was speaking the truth than any of his hearers. I am anticipating, of course, since these peculiarities did not evince themselves sufficiently to be characteristic dur-

ing this our first interview; but I had
seen enough of his lordship, before he retired to his dressing-room, to convince
me that he was something quite different
from what I had imagined. Pompous perhaps he was, but certainly neither a bore
nor stupid. In fact, I felt both pleased
and grateful to him; for he had already
given me an outline sketch for one of
my *dramatis personæ*, in a play which, as
usual, I happened at the time to have in
hand.

But if my conjectures had proved fal-
lacious as to his lordship, they had gone
infinitely more astray with respect to his
wife. I had looked for a Mrs. Siddons or
a Miss O'Neill. I found—well—a lady of
plump proportions indeed, and (as I knew
from my father's mouth) of mature age,
but—at least by candle-light—a fairy; a
bright and beautiful being, with eyes that
absolutely danced with vivacity; rounded
limbs that never stirred except with grace;

a voice that filled the air with sweetness;
a carriage like that of Juno, when it pleased
her to *be* Juno, but more often like that of
Venus. Her dress was cut exceedingly low.
('I never!' was Aunt Ben's muttered ejaculation when her ladyship first swam into
the room, and certainly *I* had never.) Her
light-brown hair, of which she had an immense quantity, fell over her bare shoulders, and shone like gold, as it well might,
for it was powdered with gold-dust.

'How French!' said Aunt Ben.

'How beautiful!' said I, when we talked
of her that night.

'You are both right,' was my father's
witty rejoinder, 'for she is Paris and Helen
in one person.'

Though her ladyship bore her years like
a feather, she would not, doubtless, have
looked so young, had it not been for the
contrast she presented to her husband; but
by the side of that ancient fowl she seemed
quite a spring chicken. He was evidently

exceedingly proud of her, and crowed feebly
over the admiration she excited; but of
that which gave her interest in my eyes—
the fact of her having been an ornament of
the British stage — he was by no means
proud. This was made evident within the
first quarter of an hour.

As my father was taking her in to dinner, she stopped in the hall, to admire its
vast proportions.

'What a capital place it would be,
Mr. Wray, for private theatricals! The
stage would have three practicable doors—
which is most unusual—and the gallery
is already there, in your magnificent staircase.'

She made nothing of stopping the whole
procession behind her, and imperilling the
warmth of the soup, while she uttered these
observations, which, however, made my
heart leap within me.

'I am sure,' said I audaciously, 'if you
were to ask my father, Lady Repton, he

would not refuse to test the capabilities of the hall as a theatre.'

'Is he so very good-natured?' said her ladyship, looking from him to me with quite an eager air. 'There is nothing in the world I should enjoy so much.'

'What, what, what?' exclaimed the old lord apprehensively, as he toddled up with Aunt Ben. 'What does she want now?'

'Lady Repton has expressed a wish, which, I am sure, shall be gratified as far as lies in my power,' said my father graciously, 'to see some private theatricals in our hall.'

'Private fiddlesticks!' ejaculated his lordship hastily. 'Very difficult, very ridiculous! Who is to act, I should like to know?'

'*I* will act!' exclaimed Lady Repton, with a sweep of her rounded arm, and in the tones of the Tragic Muse. 'There will be nothing very ridiculous in that, I hope.'

'My *dear* Lady Repton,' expostulated

the old lord, 'the idea is preposterous. I
won't have Fred Wray's hall pulled all to
pieces—I won't indeed. Carpets up, cur-
tains torn, servants drunk, and house set
on fire—that's what is meant by private
theatricals. Pooh, pooh!'

'He's afraid of my going on the stage
again and being fallen in love with,' said
her ladyship slyly, and squeezing my father's
arm. 'It *is* so hard on me, to whom the
smell of the footlights is like a breath of
fresh air.'

Nothing more was said upon the matter
at that time, though I, for my part, was
well resolved it should not drop out of
mind. But what had passed caused the
stream of conversation at dinner to turn
into a theatrical channel, in spite of Lord
Repton's endeavour to dam it, and though
he *did* damn it under his breath.

'Did you ever chance to see me, Miss
Wray,' asked her ladyship, addressing Aunt
Ben, 'at the Garden or the Lane?'

Aunt Ben opened her round eyes to their fullest extent, and smiled an embarrassed smile. If Lady Repton had said '*in the garden*,' she would have replied unhesitatingly, 'No;' but the use of the word 'at' informed her that something was intended beyond what met the ear.

'I played Desdemona at both houses,' continued her ladyship in explanation.

'Of course, of course,' exclaimed my aunt; 'how stupid of me! I remember now what a treat you gave us all. Let me see; it was the very year when Fred here'—she was just about to say 'was born,' but fortunately stopped herself, as with a sharp curb, and substituted—'had the measles.'

'Then *you* never saw me, Mr. Frederick?' said her ladyship, turning towards me with a sweet smile.

I felt, beneath the table, Cecil's foot press mine with mischievous emphasis. I knew that I had scarcely, as the phrase goes, 'been born or thought of,' when

Kitty Conway had retired from the stage, and exchanged her tinsel crown for a real coronet; and it was only by a great effort of self-command that I was able to reply with gravity: 'I have never been inside a theatre, Lady Repton, nor so much as even to London.'

'How I envy you!' sighed she. 'What pleasures await you!—My dear Lord Repton, do you hear what our young friend says? He has never seen a play.'

'Hum—ha!' muttered her husband, so gruffly, that the tone almost implied that he wished he had never seen one either.— 'Do you grow your own mutton, Wray? This haunch is capital.'

'And your cousin there,' continued her ladyship, motioning towards Cecil, 'is he in the same pastoral state of innocence as to the drama?'

'O no,' said Cecil; 'I am an old stager.'

'What an impudent young fellow!' cried

she. 'I daresay that's what he calls me. But that shows me he can act. It is necessary for an actor to be impudent; while, on the other hand, all good actresses must be unaffected, modest, and retiring.' She laughed aloud, yet very musically, and shook her head till the gold-dust flew about it like a halo. 'Seriously, however, my dear,' continued she, addressing Jane, who was looking serious enough, and indeed morose, 'I would never advise any young lady to go upon the stage. If you feel any strong attraction to that profession—'

'I *don't*,' said Jane, opening her mouth just wide enough to emit the words, and then pursing it up again with a snap.

'That's fortunate,' said her ladyship, regarding her with great coolness; 'because it affords great temptations to vanity; and I am afraid we women are all vain. Coryton, who had "the Garden" in my time, once remarked of the profession of the stage, that it would be a charming one except for the actors and the actresses.—You remember Coryton, Lord Repton?'

'Yes.' It was plain he did, so well that he did not care to be reminded of him.

'Coryton used to play the "heavy fathers" so admirably,' continued her ladyship, 'that when I married, I got him to give me away.'

'He must have been a very generous fellow, Repton,' said my father, with a good-natured glance at her ladyship.

'Stuff and nonsense!' muttered the old gentleman angrily, and without catching the gallantry of the allusion; 'not a bit of it. Deuced lavish with other people's property; that's all.'

I thought my father would have choked. His sense of courtesy contended nobly with his sense of humour; but during the struggle, his eye caught mine, and then he fairly roared. Lady Repton laughed as heartily as he, pressing her handkerchief to her eyes, because, as I now conclude, her complexion was not quite suited to the passage of tears.

She was certainly a very good-humoured woman, but, as sometimes happens, not good-natured, or rather only good-natured as regards men. She was bitter against her own sex, probably because, in her own case, she had found them to be censorious. Jane and she had many sharp encounters together: the one, all gauze and glitter, reminded me of a dragon-fly with a sting in its tail; the other, so dark and sombre, of a water-beetle, furnished with a pair of sharp pincers that had no respect for the peerage. Their contest began at once. After dinner, her ladyship sat down at the piano, and favoured us with some bright French chansons, which she sang with great sprightliness of manner.

'That woman,' whispered Cousin Jane in my ear, 'sings like a singing chambermaid;' a criticism (I was compelled to own to myself) as accurate as it was severe.

Presently, Jane took her place at the instrument to accompany Cecil, who played the flute a little, and her ladyship came and sat by me.

'When is it to be, Mr. Fred?' inquired she behind her fan.

'When is *what* to be?' returned I with genuine innocence.

'O, come; do you suppose I am blind? Cousins are not within the prohibited degrees, we know; and I suppose she is as rich as Crœsus.'

I laughed almost aloud, so that the musician looked round from her playing with a displeased air; the idea of my marrying Cousin Jane tickled me so excessively.

'She is not at all rich,' said I; 'and you are quite mistaken in your other supposition.'

'Of course that follows, if my premises are wrong,' said her ladyship coolly. 'But it really true that you are not engaged?

I have no right to pry into your secrets,'
added she, with amazing quickness (where-
by I knew that she had seen my colour
rise) ; 'I was of course only referring to
the Begum.'

I thought this both rude and cruel, and
made no reply; but she went on quite un-
concernedly.   'Lord Repton and I concluded the affair had been arranged, and
that she was here on purpose.   I am glad
that we were wrong; at least if I were
you, I should much prefer to marry your
aunt.   What makes her — I mean your
cousin—so dull and discontented, and also
so uncivil?   She never says thank you to
anybody.   I call her *La Belle Dame sans
Merci.'*

'Do you?' said I, unable to repress a
smile.   'And I heard you tell Cecil that
my father was like dear Don Quixote.   May
I ask what you call *me?*'

'Well, I shall call you Fred, if you will
let me, and if others will let me ;' and here

she gave a meaning glance towards Cousin Jane. 'You have not answered my question yet, you know. Let us suppose it's a riddle. Why is Cousin Jane so dull and discontented? Come, guess.'

'My dear Lady Repton,' said I, 'you are too severe. My cousin is an orphan, and among persons who, with one exception, are comparative strangers to her—'

'That's just my case,' interrupted her ladyship; 'yet I'm not dull.'

'That is evident,' said I gallantly.

'O, I don't mean as to wits,' continued she; 'your cousin is sharp enough—keen as a razor, I should say, and perhaps quite as dangerous. But is it possible that you can't guess my riddle?'

'Not I, indeed: I give it up.'

'You are very stupid, Mr. Fred, or else a sad hypocrite, which is almost as bad. You know when a door is not a door, I suppose? — Good. You know also when Love is deformed, I daresay?'

'When it's all on one side,' said I.

'Very good. Then, why is Cousin Jane
dull and discontented?—There, I see you
have it at last. The idea of a young fellow
—who writes plays too—not knowing when
a girl is in love with him.' Here the music
ceased.—'O, *thank* you, Miss Wray; that
is most beautiful indeed. Do, pray, play
us something else.'

But *La Belle Dame sans Merci* was deaf
to her entreaties, and, regardless of the visitors, got out as usual her Chinese puzzle.

CHAPTER VII.

CALL ME 'KITTY.'

LADY REPTON was one of those women who never come down to breakfast, or are seen by anybody but their waiting-maids, until the day is far advanced. Many ladies in her position do the like; but had she never married a peer, and remained Kitty Conway all her life, she would still have been a late riser. This habit was now an advantage to her; it gave her the opportunity of repairing the ravages of time, and presenting as bold a front as possible—and some of her own sex averred it was very bold—to the public eye: she appeared at once all smiles and pleasantness; not stiff and formal, as even the most charming

women sometimes will be under the chill
influence of morning—for breakfast-time
is a most trying epoch—but resumed the
friendly intercourse of the preceding evening
exactly at the point where it was broken
off. Though it was obvious, even under
these favourable circumstances, that she
was not without obligations to art, this
was only so far as her personal attractions
were concerned. She thoroughly understood that naturalness of manner, provided
one is not by nature a fool nor a brute,
is the greatest of social charms; that courtesy and politeness being understood, there
is indeed nothing so attractive; and accordingly, out of the abundance of her
heart did her pretty mouth speak. Thereby, Kitty Conway had doubtless 'shocked'
a large section of society during her somewhat checkered career; but she had en-
deared herself to that portion of it which
it was most worth her while (and every
lady's while) to please. Even Aunt Ben,

who had at first been certainly among the 'shocked,' was brought to confess of Lady Repton, that she didn't believe there 'was *much* real harm in her,' though she always stuck to it that there was some.

Almost the first words Lady Repton spoke to me that day were, 'And now, Mr. Fred, where are these great plays of yours?' For which I could have kissed her, and I don't think she would have been much offended if I had.

'Let us go somewhere where we can be quite alone,' said she, 'and read them.'

I took her to Aunt Ben's boudoir— which, notwithstanding its name, was rarely used except by her favourite cat, who sat there whenever a fire was lighted—and produced my chosen manuscripts with a beating heart. Of course they were crude productions, and had very little originality; but I had at least copied from the best models, and the result astonished and delighted her.

'Why, my dear Mr. Fred,' cried she, when she had read out a passage or two, which I had specially selected for her, 'you are quite a genius!'

I blushed, and bowed.

'And do you really think there would be any chance of my getting them acted?'

'These?—as they are?' said her lady-ship, laying her taper fingers upon the precious pile. 'Certainly not, unless there is a theatre at Hanwell or Bedlam. No sane man would think of putting on his stage a play in which there are no carpen-ter's scenes.'

'Carpenter's scenes!' repeated I, my mind at once reverting to the wood-yard; 'why carpenter's?'

How merrily she laughed! The laugh-ter of no child was ever blither or more musical than hers; and yet, for fear it should have displeased me, she became at once supernaturally grave, and entered into explanation.

'You don't give your hero and heroine time to dress, Mr. Fred, nor scarcely to breathe; while as for the necessities of the scenery, you have ignored that altogether. You would have done very well in the old days, when a man came on, and said, "This is a wood," or, "Please to imagine a room in the king's palace;" but now-a-days, when woods and palaces are actually set up, you must give time for their erection by means of carpenter's scenes. In a literary point of view, my dear boy'— and here she patted me on the head— 'these plays, considering your youth, are prodigies of excellence; but as dramatic works they are—well, ahem!—unadapted for representation. In the first place, you have too many good characters; I don't mean virtuous ones, for that would indeed be fatal, but individual personifications. To play these would require actors and actresses of which no company possesses more than one or two. Don't you see?'

I didn't see at all.

'Surely,' said I, 'in Shakespeare's plays, for instance, there are not one or two characters only, and the rest dummies.'

'That was the great mistake of Shakespeare,' replied her ladyship coolly. 'He was too great a man to write plays for representation, and that is why they are so much read and so seldom acted. When I played Desdemona, which I did both at the Garden and the Lane' (this piece of information may for the future be taken as spoken, though *I* heard it about a hundred times), 'there was a pretty good Othello, except that he only came up to my shoulder, and I could have smothered *him* with ease; but our Iago was a fool. Shakespeare's men, upon the whole, are wiser than his women, and that is another practical mistake of his; for very few wise men ever take to the stage as a profession. The true reason why what are now called Sensation Plays are so popular is, because

they rely upon the scene-painters, who are
excellent, and upon strong " situations,"
which suit everybody who can strike an
attitude, fall without hurting himself, or
die in convulsions. It is from the same
cause, at least so far as the managers are
concerned, that leg-pieces are so popular.'

'Dear me!' said I, not wishing farther
to expose my ignorance by inquiring into
the nature of ' leg-pieces.'

'All this,' continued her ladyship, ' I
daresay destroys your illusions respecting
the British stage; and yet I do assure you
that if anything were to happen to Lord
Repton—which heaven forbid!—I would
go back to it to-morrow.'

'I wish you would,' said I mechanically,
forgetting the domestic calamity that must
needs precede her doing so in my desire to
have a friend so potent behind the scenes.
'How I should like to see you act in—in
anything!'

'You selfish boy!' cried her ladyship,

shaking her jewelled finger in rebuke; 'you were going to say, " in one of my plays." Well, why shouldn't you do so? We were talking of private theatricals last night; let us get some up. Here is your adaptation of *Ivanhoe*, which is the very thing —not too long, and not too serious. I'll play Rowena.'

'My dear Lady Repton,' cried I in an ecstasy, 'you are too good!'

'I hope not,' answered she comically: 'I had almost rather be " no better than I should be."—Yes, Rowena will do very well. I will let my back-hair down, which I heard your Cousin Jane say was not my own. She must do Rebecca, I suppose; though where shall we ever find a Brian de Bois-Guilbert venturesome enough to carry her off? Do you know where to lay your hand upon a Brian?'

At the moment, I could think of nobody but 'the Alchemist,' as we called him —old Mr. Bourne. If he always kept his

visor down, he might possibly pass for the
bold Templar, although he had little of
that fiery character in his composition. He
would do anything to oblige Cecil, as I
had only too good reasons for knowing.
(It was not for *my* sake that his grand-
daughter was permitted to come to the
Manor-house so often, though she did come,
bless her! for my sake.) Lady Repton.
who knew nothing of Mr. Bourne, could,
of course, make no present objection to the
cast; and in the mean time I resolved to
look about and try and find a better man.
There was one Frank Close, a clergyman's
son, in our neighbourhood, who had broken
a leaping-pole once or twice in my company, and might break a lance, or at least
bear one, as Bois-Guilbert. Cecil, we arranged, should be Ivanhoe—to whom, as
to Rowena, a much more important part
was assigned in my dramatic version of the
story than in the original; and I myself
was to be Wamba, the son of Witless.

'We'll put it Wamba only, in the bill,' said her ladyship gravely, 'for fear your father shouldn't like it.'

I laughed, and told her how much she was mistaken in supposing my father capable of receiving annoyance from such a source; and she laughed too, but shook her head, in sign that we must agree to differ on that point.

'Your father is charming, I allow; but he is a man, and man is vain.' No argument could push her from that canon. 'Whatever man is vain about, in that he can be more easily wounded than any woman: his *amour propre* is more sensitive, and he is less forgiving.'

Although somewhat indignant, upon my father's account, at this sweeping condemnation of mankind, I did not care just then to combat Lady Repton's views; indeed, so far as myself was concerned, I am afraid I confirmed them; for the idea of getting my Rowena played, though only at Gatcombe,

by such an actress as Lady Repton, made
me feel as vain as a peacock. Her ladyship
was also greatly pleased at this notion of
reappearing in public even on our humble
stage. Our united wits were concentrated
upon the realisation of it. I felt quite sure
that the gallantry of my father would cause
him to consent to any scheme of amusement
which his guest might propose; and on this
point my companion was ready to believe
me, though she protested that if the thing
were done it would be for my sake, and not
for hers.

'You can get your father to do anything, you spoiled boy; I see *that;* and,
upon my word, I don't wonder at it, for
really, Fred, you are very nice.'

'It is very nice of you to say so,' said I
with an ingenuous blush. 'You don't know
how I have been longing to see you, Lady
Repton; and—'

'Call me Kitty,' interrupted her ladyship. 'When we are at our plays, at all

events, I will be Kitty, and you shall be
Fred. You longed to see me, did you; and
yet, when I came—you were going to say—
I turned out to be so different from what
you expected, eh?'

'Well, yes,' I stammered; 'I was going
to say that, or something like it.'

'I knew you were,' said she, smiling. 'I
daresay you pictured to yourself an awful
personage, with the airs of a tragedy queen.
"*I called for water, boy; you bring me beer!*"
and so on. I am afraid I must have disappointed you sadly, Fred.'

The pathos she threw into these last
words so melted my heart, that I know not
of what passionate compliment I might not
have been guilty. 'Indeed, Kitty—' I had
smilingly begun, when the door was opened,
and in walked Lord Repton. I protest that
I had no more idea of making love to his
lordship's wife than of stealing his wig, and
yet his sudden appearance gave me quite a
qualm, nay, a spasm of conscience, the se-

verity of which was by no means mitigated by his first words, delivered with stately disapprobation.

'I am sorry to interrupt your *tête-à-tête*, Lady Repton, but I thought that I heard somebody say "Kitty."'

'And so you did,' said her ladyship, with her musical laugh, and pointing to the hearth-rug, where the cat, aroused by the opening of the door, was stretching its legs and bending its back. 'Puss and I, as it happens, are both Kitties.'

'Hum—ha!' said his lordship, regarding the animal with a grave air. 'I had no idea that Kitty was a name of common gender, or was ever applied to a Tom-cat.'

This idea so tickled him, that he at once discarded the suspicion which had apparently suggested it, and was put in high good-humour.

'And do you really mean to say, young sir,' said he, in a bantering tone, pointing to the piles of manuscript upon the table, 'that you have spoiled all that paper with fine writing?'

'Indeed, my lord,' said her ladyship with some warmth, kindled, not so much on my account, I fancy, as because she had had a little fright upon her own, 'Mr. Frederick has not only written fine things; some of them are very good.'

'I daresay, I daresay,' replied her husband, with lofty condescension. 'I remember, when I was a lad of the same age, I was always writing too. The things may have been nothing of themselves, but I had no cause to be ashamed of them: they showed culture. In after-years, though you may not have chanced to hear of it, young gentleman, I had some little reputation as a dramatic critic.'

'Indeed, I have heard my father say so many times, my lord,' said I submissively. 'If I could venture to ask your opinion now upon these humble efforts—'

I had fished for perch in a shower, but

I had never seen a bait swallowed so greed-
ily as was this adroit suggestion of mine by
my noble friend. He had sat himself down,
and fastened his gold spectacles upon his
aristocratic nose, before I could finish the
sentence.

Nothing would please him better, he
said, than to place his poor services as a
critic at the disposal of a son of his valued
friend.

My heart so smote me for my hypocrisy
that I could only murmur some disjointed
words of thanks, and push the manuscripts
towards him. We should, without doubt,
have been in for a lecture on the Unities,
had not woman's wit come to the rescue,
and shaped the threatened infliction into a
weapon wherewith to win the very thing
on which our hearts were set.

'Why don't you ask Lord Repton's
opinion upon the matter we were discuss-
ing?' said her ladyship as she kneeled on
the hearth-rug smoothing the cat. 'Let

him decide whether your *Elfrida* or your *Ivanhoe* is most suitable for our dramatic representation.'

'What, what, what?' said the old lord in a fretful tone.

'Why, you must know that we are going to have some private theatricals at Gatcombe,' continued she: 'Mr. Wray has set his heart upon giving his neighbours a little treat in that way, and I have promised to help him.'

'Not to *act*, Lady Repton, I do hope?'

'Well, that is as you please, my lord, of course. I had hoped you would have consented to my doing myself the great pleasure of stabbing Mr. Frederick in the back as he sat upon his pony—we could easily get the pony into the hall—on the point of his departure from Corfe Castle.'

'I shall certainly forbid your doing anything so supremely absurd, and—and—unbecoming, Lady Repton.'

'There! didn't I tell you so?' said her

ladyship, appealing despondingly to me.
'And it's *such* a pity! because I know I
could make something out of a part like
Elfrida's; whereas, in the other play, the
character of Rowena is merely a sketch,
hardly worth the trouble of letting one's
back-hair down for, in order to look the
part.'

'I object to your acting *at all*, Lady
Repton,' said her husband, taking at the
same time, however, into his trembling
hand the *Ivanhoe* which I respectfully ten-
dered.

'I knew it, my lord, and I·said so,'
returned her ladyship plaintively. 'I did
not even venture to promise myself that
innocent pleasure. But I am sure you will
not put a stop to our projected amusement
altogether, by refusing me permission to aid
the young folks here by saying half-a-dozen
words in what is, after all, but a child's
play. You are too good-natured to do that,
I am sure.'

'But why the deuce can't they play the thing without you, madam?' inquired the old lord, still testily, but not without signs of yielding in his tone.

'Because, my dear Lord Repton,' said her ladyship, taking his unwilling hand and folding it in her abundant tresses, 'there is nobody here who looks like a Saxon princess except me. Miss Wray is rather a brunette, you see; whereas Rowena was a blonde, as I am. There will not be the least occasion for any theatrical costume. I shall wear the diamond tiara you were so good as to give me, with my white silk; leave my chair for the mimic stage, which will be no stage at all, to say the few words that have been assigned to me, and then return to your side. Indeed, we should never have troubled you about the matter, only we wished to have your opinion upon some dramatic points; for whatever is worth doing at all, as I was telling Mr. Frederick, is worth doing well.'

Here a pebble struck the window; and upon my rising to answer a signal commonly employed by my father when he wished to attract my attention from without, I saw him standing in the garden.

'I must positively forbid your boring both my guests, Fred, or at least both at one time,' said he, 'with your dramatic compositions. They tell me you have got Lord Repton up there as well as her ladyship, and I insist upon your releasing him without ransom. Tell him I want a good Yorkshire opinion upon my new cob.'

'Yes, yes,' said the old lord, appearing at the open window; 'I'll come, I'll come. I've some little reputation as a judge of horse-flesh, and I believe it is merited.—I'll look over your play in the evening, Mr. Frederick;' and off he went.

'We must take care he does not do that,' said her ladyship comically—'Kit, Kit, Kittie;' and then she began to laugh immoderately. 'My dear Mr. Fred, what a scrape we were very nearly in!'

But, notwithstanding Lady Repton's modest resolve to wear only her own white silk as the Saxon Rowena, she was very solicitous that the rest of the *dramatis personæ* should be suitably attired; and it was arranged before we left the boudoir that an embassy should be sent to Monkton to hire the necessary dresses at the theatre. We took my father's consent to our dramatic entertainment for granted, though, in due time, Lady Repton did not fail to thank him for it. He was considerably astonished, but much too polite to offer any objection beyond shaking his fist at me.

'You must go and break this news, sir, to Aunt Ben,' said he. 'It is she who is Lord Chamberlain, and from whom your license must issue.' But he went with us, for all that, to back our humble petition.

'I am sure I will do all I can,' said my aunt, looking at him doubtfully; 'but—I don't pretend to know anything of play-acting—but won't they hurt the hall?'

'They will probably burn down the house, my dear,' was my father's encouraging reply. Then he looked at me, and quoted from his favourite Marlowe :

> 'The northern borderers, seeing their houses burn'd,
> Their wives and children slain, run up and down,
> Cursing the names of *thee and Lady Repton*.'

Her ladyship clapped her hands, delighted. 'Perhaps Mr. Wray would act himself?' suggested she in a stage-whisper.

'I trust he will not dream of acting anybody else,' exclaimed Aunt Ben hastily.

'Don't you think we could persuade him to play Bois-Guilbert, in place of this Mr. Bourne?' observed her ladyship insinuatingly, and without noticing my aunt's indignant protest.

'What Mr. Bourne?' inquired my father. —'You don't mean to say, Fred, that you have proposed to put the rector into chain-armour?'

'No, sir,' said I modestly. 'I meant Mr. Bourne the elder.'

'Worse and worse!' cried he. 'Why, he's nearly eighty; though, I daresay,' added my father under his breath, 'he'd be happy to come for a shilling a night and his supper.'

'Eighty!' exclaimed Lady Repton in her turn: 'what Rebecca in the world will stand being made love to by a man of eighty! How dare you, Mr. Fred!'

Then I had to explain that I had merely suggested Mr. Bourne in order not to throw any difficulties in the way of our scheme at starting; but that I felt sure Frank Close would play the part—as indeed he eventually did. Lady Repton did not fail, however, to reproach me, the next time we were alone together, for this audacious duplicity.

'You will say anything to gain your ends, it seems, you wicked boy. I have altered my good opinion of you altogether. How do I know that we have even secured a Rebecca? Are you quite sure that your Cousin Jane will act?'

'I am quite sure that she will not,' said I, laughing.

'Well, that's pleasant hearing, I must say; but I hope you see your way out of the difficulty.'

'Yes,' said I. 'There's a young neighbour of ours—you'll see her to-night at dinner — Miss Eleanor Bourne; I am sure she will oblige us in the matter, and she will look the part to perfection.'

'Then she must be very beautiful,' observed her ladyship sharply.

'She is thought to be good-looking,' returned I coolly, 'and she is very dark.' And thus we settled it.

Now all was bustle and preparation; and Aunt Ben busied herself in writing the invitations, for there was no time to lose, since the Reptons' stay with us was to be very short. It was decided that a dress rehearsal should take place, for the amuse-

ment of our humbler friends in the village,
on the day before the grand entertainment,
and in the mean while there was much to
do.   Cecil copied out the parts; Lady
Repton suggested the arrangements for the
stage; and my father loosened his purse-
strings cheerfully.   I don't think I was ever
before so happy, though I felt a little dis-
concerted that same evening when welcoming Eleanor in Lady Repton's presence.

'So *that* is the young neighbour of
yours, is it, Master Fred,' said she slyly,
'who is "thought to be good-looking"!   I
shall find an opportunity of telling her after
dinner what you said of her.   "Very dark."
Yes; and I think you have kept her very
dark from *me*.'

'I forgot that you knew nothing about
her,' said I, with rather an awkward laugh;
'Eleanor is a very old friend of ours.'

'So it seems,' said her ladyship dryly.   'I
observe that you squeeze hands.'

Old Mr. Bourne was certainly right in

the remark he expressed that night (if not
in the pronunciation of it), that Lady Repton had 'the heye of a nawk.'

But though I do verily believe that she
was displeased for the moment to discover
that Nelly and I were lovers, she took to
her very kindly, and they soon got to be
excellent friends.

CHAPTER VIII.

DRAMATIC PREPARATIONS.

WHAT a revolution can one person of wit
and will effect in a whole household, however prone to peace and lethargy! The
silent Manor-house now resounded to the
blows of the carpenter, as though it had
been one of her Majesty's dockyards, while
provisions arrived (for the contemplated
supper) in stores as if to furnish forth an
Arctic expedition. Aunt Ben, ordinarily so
phlegmatic, positively simmered with excitement and sense of responsibility; and
even Cousin Jane bestirred herself to the
extent of volunteering to hear our parts.
In the case of Lady Repton herself, no such
tutoring was supposed to be necessary; and

indeed she had boasted to me that she was a most excellent 'study;' but disuse, I fancy, had somewhat affected her powers in this way; for she was never without her scraps of paper, and in the middle of a conversation would suddenly reply to one in the mediæval style, and give the cue with immense significance. At church, too, in the Wray pew (as it was called)—a little curtained snuggery in the gallery, which might well have excused the impropriety, as reminding her of a stage-box—she was wont to mix up with the responses certain tags and phrases which were sometimes longer than the sentences for which they were substituted, and overlapped them, so to speak, in a most extraordinary and indecorous manner. Nothing was said about it, though my father raised his eyebrows a little, and Aunt Ben lifted her hands in horror. It was generally understood that her ladyship did not ' mean anything wrong.' Certainly, that was my view of her conduct, and still is, though I had a much greater experience of her eccentricities than the rest of the household. At this distance of time, it will be thought neither a breach of confidence nor an act of vanity to confess that her ladyship made downright love to me. But she was perfectly well aware that it was an absurd thing to do, and occasionally burst out laughing in the middle of it. 'One may not marry one's grandmother, Fred, nor even fall in love with her,' she would say, as if to reassure me, when matters seemed to be going a little far; or, 'What sad lines time has ruled in my old face,' when she had been putting it unnecessarily close to mine. That there was no reality in her little endearments, I think I could almost have convinced Nelly herself. I don't believe she was even 'keeping her hand in' for that time which she vaguely spoke of as 'when anything should happen to dear Lord Repton;' but she was a born actress, devoted to love-making on the stage,

and was content to play Helena even to so
cruel a Demetrius as myself. No flower-
juice on earth could have ever made me
blind to Nelly, or to look on 'Kitty' with
any other eyes than those of the most
modest, though affectionate, regard. Her
conversation, however, at all times delighted
me, and especially when she spoke of dramatic matters, which generally formed the
topic of our talk. Her wit, therefore, must
have been great indeed, since she did not
hesitate to damp my hopes of succeeding
as a playwright, and even of my getting
'acted' at all. 'If Shakespeare himself had
not had a share in the Globe Theatre, my
dear, he would not have been the great
success he was, for the simple reason, that
he would not have had the opportunities.
The stage-door is not more closed against
the general public than is the manager's
ear to the voice of the unknown writer of
dramas. He won't be bothered with him,
not even so far as to give him a hearing.

He will answer no notes, however courte-
ous; he will return no manuscript, however
valuable.'

'Then a manager must be a brute in
human form!' cried I indignantly.

'Undoubtedly he is, my dear boy,' was
her grave reply; 'if at least he is so fortunate as to possess the human form, for I
have known some managers without even
that: being intensely selfish, they hate
trouble of all kinds; and they have an in-
surmountable objection to spend money.
These two peculiarities cause them to ac-
cept French adaptations, written by hack
writers, in place of good original dramas,
that they would be put to the pains of se-
lecting from a heap of literary rubbish, and
for which, perhaps, they might have to pay
a reasonable sum.'

'But how, then, is an unknown dramatic author to get his chance at all?'

'By writing his play expressly to suit
the capabilities of a particular actor or ac-

tress, and getting him or her to bring it
out for him—just as I am now bringing
out your *Ivanhoe* for you upon the Gatcombe stage. Only, all the profession, my
dear Fred, are not so good-natured, I assure you. A gentleman of my acquaintance once wrote a very charming comedy
upon an express understanding with X, a
certain eminent actor, that he should bring
out the piece; the principal part was exactly suited to his talents, and he had even
allowed that the play was sure to take.
But still it remained unacted. At last the
author lost patience, and demanded an explanation. " I have been kept shilly-shal-
lying long enough," said he (just as you
will be, my dear Fred), " and really begin
to think that this play is not coming out at
all. I would rather give a hundred pounds
than be disappointed in this way." "My
dear friend," returned X in his friendly
way, "why on earth did you not say so
before ? That is the very thing—I mean

your hundred pounds—for which (from
motives of delicacy) I have so patiently
been waiting." '

'What a villain !' ejaculated I.

'Perhaps,' said her ladyship coolly; 'but
a very smiling and agreeable villain, I do
assure you.'

While the general conditions of the
British stage were thus being expounded to
my astonished ears, no pains were spared
to insure the success of that particular
ornament of it, my mediæval drama —
or, to speak technically, to make *Ivanhoe*
'go.' We had already had more than one
rehearsal; and upon a certain Thursday,
the date of which became afterwards of
very serious importance, Cecil and I started
for Monkton, to hire the dresses. They
could not be procured before, for the simple
reason, that the Thespian wardrobe in the
cathedral city was limited, and that the
actors were using them ; but the company
was now disbanded, and the manager was

glad enough to turn an honest pound or
two by us amateurs.

It was very kind of my cousin to go
with me, at a time when all studies, save
our dramatic ones, were suspended; and
he would, as I well knew, have gladly
spent his holiday elsewhere; but, of course,
not a word was said of *that*. The subject,
as I have said, was a tabooed one, and indeed it did not at that time even suggest
itself to me.

The behaviour of Cousin Jane had of
late been so conciliatory, that it had in a
great measure removed my suspicions of
her having discovered her brother's secret,
and besides, my mind was full of the play.
My astonishment, therefore, was considerable when suddenly, as we drove along,
Cecil observed, apropos to nothing: 'What
a charming Rowena my Rue would make,
Fred!'

His quiet use of the possessive pronoun
alarmed me more than the most passionate

eulogy on her beauty could have done. *His*
Rue, indeed! Why I couldn't have said
more if I had been speaking of my own
Eleanor! 'Well,' returned I, smiling, for
I thought it best to treat the matter as
lightly as I could, 'I don't suppose Ruth
Waller would play the part so well as
Lady Repton.'

'I am not sure,' answered he gravely;
'she would *look* the Saxon princess every
inch, and she has far more dramatic talent
than you imagine.'

'But I never imagined her to have *any*,
my dear Cecil,' returned I in astonishment.
'How should she have? What could have
evoked it?'

Cecil laughed—not scornfully, but with
the good-natured confidence of a man whose
position is beyond ridicule. 'Well, Fred,
I might reply,' said he, 'if I had a mind
to be uncivil, How came *you* with your
knack of writing plays? And, Who evoked
that?'

'I should answer, Cecil, that my reading of plays begat my writing them; partly that, and partly, I suppose, I must have had some natural bent that way at first, which, it is likely enough, might never have shown itself but for my father's encouragement. Why, at seven years old I used to sit on his knee, and, drawing a paper-knife, speak Macbeth's speech : " Is this a dagger that I see before me ?"'

'Well,' said Cecil, 'and I have taught Rue.'

'Not sitting on your knee,' laughed I, 'I hope!—Pardon me, my dear cousin,' I added hastily, for it was plain to see that I had offended him. 'Indeed, I meant no harm. Ruth Waller is a good girl, I know; but it does seem to me so very strange that she should be capable of acting in a stage-play.'

'Why not?' returned he coldly. 'Talents are not given to us in proportion to our riches, else I should be cleverer than my sister Jane; and as to birth, does not your father's favourite Bianca say :

" Mean folks are as worthy
To be well spoken of, if they deserve well,
As some whose only fame lies in their blood !"

Or hear Ben Jonson :

" We stand too much on our gentility,
Which is an airy and mere borrow'd thing
From dead men's dust and bones, and none of ours,
Except we make or hold it." '

My cousin's tone had a certain scornful fire I had never before noticed in it; and for which, though I regretted the source that kindled it, I admired him none the less. It was doubtless very foolish of him to have taken up with this beautiful beggar-maid; but others, thought I, besides King Cophetua had been similarly infatuated: for it must be remembered, that though I had played the mentor in this matter with much becoming gravity, I was then but eighteen myself.

'Of course,' said I, 'my dear Cecil, I

agree with every word of that: there is
nothing so despicably Brummagem as the
rubbish that is talked about Birth: but
just as the associations that belong to your
noble swell from his earliest years are disadvantageous, just as he is liable to be
spoiled by flattery and the habit of having
his own way—and *is* spoiled—for he generally grows up to be a fool—so is your
poor lad, and more especially your poor
girl, begirt from the first by associations
of an opposite kind, but at least equally
disadvantageous to *them*.   It is not Ruth
Waller's fault, for instance, that she is familiar with certain scenes that—to say the
least of them — must tend to vulgarise a
woman's nature.'

'Ruth's nature is not vulgar,' observed
Cecil curtly.

I shrugged my shoulders, and flicked
the pony with the whip.

'It is useless to argue the matter, Cecil,'
said I presently; 'you might as well con-

tend, on the other hand, that the born swells are wise: when they are so, they are miracles, that's all. Perhaps Ruth Waller is a miracle; for your sake I hope she is— How fine the cathedral tower begins to look!'

'Never mind the cathedral, Fred. Listen to me; you are the only friend I have in the world. What are the " certain scenes" with which you say Ruth has been of necessity familiar, and that must needs have done her harm?'

'Well,' said I, 'scenes of drunkenness, for instance. It is impossible it can be otherwise. I have myself seen Richard Waller as drunk as a pig within these few days.'

'Yes,' replied Cecil sorrowfully, 'it is terrible. She does what she can to keep him sober, but it is hopeless. He is diligent enough, but the half of what he earns is spent in drink. Well' (here he spoke with cheerful gravity, like one who has

weighed all the disadvantages to be en-
countered in a design, and still is fixed),
' of *that* wretchedness at least—I mean their
poverty—there will be no more when Rue
is mine.'

'It is a sad look-out,' said I, ' nevertheless, to have a drunkard for a brother-in-
law.'

'True,' returned Cecil; 'but you do not
value the compensation as I do. You do
not know Ruth. Her beauty is her least
recommendation.'

' She is certainly most beautiful,' said I.

' Ah, yes; there is no one like her —
none.'

In his mind's eye, it was evident the
boy beheld her; his face grew radiant, his
tone became bright and joyous; and by the
time we reached Monkton, he was in higher
spirits than I had ever known him. He
seemed resolved to forget all his trouble in
the mission on which we were bent; while
as for me, it, of course, gave me an intense

pleasure. I shall never forget the amusement our visit to that little dusty, musty
theatre afforded us; the first edifice of the
sort into which I had ever set foot; so different from everything I had heard or pictured to myself of the Temple of Thespis;
the stage with the gilt off with a vengeance! The little ' 'Ebrew Jew,' its proprietor, did away with my illusions more
completely, however, than even the establishment itself. He was humility and
insignificance personified; and seemed as
incapable of rejecting a drama from anybody as of accepting one; and yet, he was
a real live manager—when there was anything to manage, which did not always
happen, dramatic affairs at Monkton being
very intermittent. His great object appeared to be to persuade us to hire certain
wigs which he exhibited, one by one, with
excessive pride. They were not so attractive in themselves as to induce us to wear
them for our private use, while for a me-

diæval drama they were clearly inappro-
priate. He had evidently, however, never
even so much as heard of an anachronism,
and combated that objection with great
vigour. In private theatricals, he contended that the most important thing of all
was to conceal your personal identity; and
there was nothing so certain to effect this
object as wigs. Eventually, to please him,
we did hire a magnificent wig and beard
for Isaac, Rebecca's father, who was not
represented in the drama at all. We got
a very tolerable suit of armour for Bois-
Guilbert, not much above two sizes larger
than Frank Close, who was to wear it; and
a palmer's cloak—which I suspect was used
at funerals in the town—for Ivanhoe. As
for myself, I secured a most marvellous
jester's suit in which to appear as Wamba.
It was of a light salmon colour, and formed
of some elastic woollen material in one
piece. When I had crept into it, it was
fastened behind by two buttons, and there

I was, dependent for subsequent deliverance upon the charity of my friends. If
I could only be half so funny in speech as I
was to look at, the success of the comic
business of the drama was undoubtedly
secured.

Laden with these garments, and much
other tinselled spoil besides, we returned to
Gatcombe, to exhibit them to the admiring
household. Even Lord Repton expressed
his satisfaction upon the whole, although,
had he gone with us, the result would have
been, doubtless, even still more successful.
' He had some reputation,' it seemed, as a
judge of mediæval costume, which could not
have failed to have been useful to us.

Cousin Jane alone absented herself from
the display of our borrowed plumes. She
had complained of headache, it was said,
and had shut herself up in her room all
day, where she had requested that she
might not be disturbed.

For the rest of us, it was an evening of

great excitement, for the dress rehearsal, to
which the farmers and principal village
folk had been invited, was to come off on
the ensuing afternoon.   How little we
guessed that in place of our modest little
drama there was to be performed—a Tragedy!

CHAPTER IX.

A TRAGEDY AFTER A FARCE.

At breakfast the next morning, Lady Repton, for a wonder, made her appearance; but Jane kept her room, as she had done throughout the preceding day, still troubled with her headache. I am afraid this did not interfere with the merriment of our party, reinforced as it was by the presence of Eleanor, whom we had bespoken for the entire day. Nothing, of course, was talked about but the afternoon's rehearsal, and quotations from the play were frequent, which, interspersed with ordinary talk, had a comic effect enough. To my father, however, must be adjudged the palm of electrifying the company, and especially Aunt Ben, by his application, to my own un-

happy condition as playwright, of these
lines from Marlowe's *Faustus*, uttered suddenly in sad and sonorous tones :

'O Frederick,
Now hast thou but six bare hours to live,
And then thou wilt be damn'd perpetually.'

Though spoken in jest, these words did not
tend to remove the nervousness which had
taken possession of me, and it was with a
ghastly grin that I acknowledged the sally.
Mere gibes and jokes, so long as they did
not take this Cassandra shape, I did not
mind; which was fortunate, for no one
spared me. Cecil boldly addressed the
most affectionate speeches to Eleanor before my face, under the borrowed shield of
Bois - Guilbert; and Lady Repton lavished
upon Cecil all the tenderness (and something more) with which I had endowed
Rowena. Then she would turn to me, and
ejaculate : 'Poor faithful fool!' with such
contemptuous pity that Aunt Ben got
quite indignant upon my account. When

Frank Close arrived, and we all put on our costumes, the fun became positively uproarious. His head-gear was so much too large for him that his eyes, which should have 'flashed fire through his visor bars,' were lost somewhere between that spot and his mouthpiece, so that he could see nothing, and had to be led about. As for me in my salmon suit, I was thoroughly ashamed of myself, and looked very much of the same colour as my apparel. Frank Close, too, whose humour was of a practical turn, did not mend matters—and, indeed, he did precisely the reverse, for he made a hole in my inexpressibles—by perpetually prodding my unprotected limbs with his sword. The three male characters of the drama, indeed, were faint and sore with laughter before they emerged from the 'green-room' and presented themselves to the public eye. Our two actresses excited nothing but admiration, while their costumes were perfection. Lady Repton really looked superb, notwithstanding that the remorseless light of day fell full upon her; and the beauty of Rebecca was (as Rowena herself confessed) such as to have excused any indiscretion on the part of the Templar.

Ah me! what a bright joyous time it was! how full of jest and gaiety! A day wherein Youth, Love, and Friendship made holiday together, and asked Wit to join them!

And yet we could scarce have been more merry or better pleased among ourselves than were those who came to gaze upon our show—the farmers of the parish, with their wives. Stout Fiveacres, whose family had held the self-same farm for centuries, and yet who was, I verily believe, the very first of them who ever saw a play; young Bargate, from the Glebe House, with his bride of three days old, whom this unprecedented attraction had withdrawn thus early from her modest seclusion; and old Braintree, from whom all his race had dropped away, except the little blue-eyed grandchild, whom he had asked special leave to bring: 'She would take up no room,' he said, 'as she always sat upon his knee.'

Not until the company had all assembled did Cousin Jane appear and take her seat in the front row beside my father. She looked ill and pale, and also nervous, as I had never seen her before.

'Your cousin appears anxious,' remarked Lady Repton.

'Yes,' said I; 'she is afraid of Cecil's coming to grief in his part, which I am sure she need not be.'

'Nay, I think she is afraid of the piece itself not going off as it should do,' answered her ladyship slyly.

'I am sure that is not it,' said I, 'for she was opposed to our having the play from the beginning.'

'Yes; for two reasons: first, because

you take the jester's part, which she con-
siders inconsistent with your dignity; and
secondly, because Eleanor plays with you.
What a terrible young fellow you are, to
have thus involved three innocent young
creatures—for you know how *I* dote upon
you—in your wicked meshes!'

Her lively ladyship retained her own
opinion on this point, as was usual with
her; but although she had been the first
to open my eyes to Cousin Jane's *penchant*
for myself, I felt convinced she was wrong
in this particular instance. Jane's present
anxiety was certainly upon Cecil's account,
not mine. Her eyes followed his every
movement; her ears seemed to await his
words alone, throughout the play; and so
far from my being chagrined at her want
of interest in the drama itself, I felt more
favourably towards her in consequence.
Whatever might be urged against Cousin
Jane, it was certain that she really loved
'Old Cecil' (as I affectionately termed him),

and was demonstrative enough in all that
concerned *him*.

At what precise part of the representation it happened, I cannot tell, for the
shock of subsequent occurrences destroyed
all recollection of such details; but it was
at a point when all the *dramatis personæ*
were on the stage together, that a strange
sensation seemed to affect the servants
on the staircase, which, as I have said,
served the purpose of a gallery. At first
there was only whispering and crowding
together; but presently one of them—it
was Anne, the parlour-maid—stood up, and
looked towards my father nervously. All
eyes in the body of the hall, including his
own, were, however, fixed upon ourselves.

'Master—sir!' said Anne.

My father looked up, in common with
every one else, at this unexpected interruption, except Cousin Jane, who still kept her
eyes fixed upon her brother, at that moment on his knees before Rowena, and

even when he looked round, she never turned her head.

'What is the matter?' asked my father gravely.

'The house is on fire; I knew it would be, Fred,' cried Aunt Ben reproachfully.

(Considering that our entertainment was an afternoon performance, and of course without footlights, it was rather unreasonable in her to attribute such a misfortune to my poor drama.)

'No, sir,' said Anne; 'it's not fire. But a terrible accident has happened at the sand-cliff; and I thought I ought to tell you.'

'To whom?' cried Cecil.

Even in that moment of increased excitement, it seemed to strike the company as strange that Cecil should have put this question instead of my father; perhaps it was the feverish anxiety of his voice, so different from the tones of tender passion in which he had just been addressing

Rowena, but, at all events, Anne turned to him, as though she had known he was the person chiefly interested.

'It's the Wallers' pit, Mr. Cecil, over against Wayford—'

The next instant there was a sharp clang of the door, and Cecil was gone. The whole audience rose at once—almost all of them to hurry to the scene of the catastrophe. My father and Aunt Ben remained but to collect the few articles which their experience had shown to be useful in such emergencies, and the *dramatis personæ* to disencumber themselves of their stage clothes. Even in that moment of distress and alarm, it was not without a sense of humorous absurdity that I found myself a prisoner in the salmon-coloured suit. I could obtain nobody's aid to undo the two buttons behind, and, in that hateful apparel, it was utterly impossible that I could present myself on the cliff terrace at such a time. It would have been a hundred times worse than going to a funeral in hunting costume. At last I procured a knife, and cut it open down the front (just as the Japanese disembowel themselves), and so got out. Then at full speed I followed, and soon passed the rest of the hurrying throng. In the avenue lay Ivanhoe's long palmer's cloak, which poor Cecil had cast off as he ran. I could see his white shirt-sleeves, as he sped along the terrace like a deer, at least half a mile ahead of me. In front of the place where Richard and Ruth Waller usually worked, I could also see a dark knot of men and women — a funereal group which seemed already to speak of death. As I drew nearer, I found these standing around the pit-mouth in a semicircle, within which, just as I arrived, a man came out from the pit with a barrowful of earth, which he emptied very hastily, and then returned. The faces of all expressed an intense anxiety and grief — not the mere curiosity which is too often the feeling chiefly recognisable in the onlookers at tragic scenes: not one of those present but had had cause to bewail a similar catastrophe on their own account, or on that of their kinsfolk.

'On whom has the pit fallen?' inquired I of one who had already stripped his coat off, in readiness to take his turn at the work within, though he was an old man too.

'On Richard Waller and his sister. sir.'

'Good God!' cried I. 'What! on Ruth?' I looked round nervously for Cecil, but he had disappeared.

'Yes, indeed, sir; though we trust the lass is not so far in but that she can be reached in time. That little lad there' (pointing to a pale-faced child, who was crying bitterly) 'was helping a bit with the barrow, when he heard the fall, and ran out to tell us. It was lucky—if anything can be called lucky in such an affair—that he was there to hear it, or we should not have known what had happened until it was too late.'

'Then you think,' asked I eagerly, 'that it is not too late now?'

'Not for the lass, sir — no; though I fear poor Richard is done for. From what the lad says, I reckon Ruth was only just beyond the props when the sand came down.'

'Beyond the props!' cried I, in amazement. 'How could that be?'

'Heaven only knows, sir; though I do fear that the drink which has led poor Richard to spend his substance, has at last cost him his life.'

'You don't mean to say that Richard Waller sold his props for drink, when he knew that his sister was to share his risk?' cried I indignantly.

'I know nothing certain, sir, except that drink will make a man sell anything, including, as Parson Bourne says, his own soul; and, at all events, the props are gone, or how could yon have happened ?'

Here the barrow-man came out, looking white and exhausted, and was immediately relieved by another hand; and a few minutes afterwards a second man emerged from the pit, for whom another was similarly substituted on the instant. Not a single second was lost. There was a total silence now, the slight commotion caused by the coming up of the party from the Manor-house having ceased. My father was standing in the inner ring of spectators, with a little pile of blankets beside him, and a bottle of brandy; one finger was in his waistcoat-pocket, where, as I well knew, a lancet lay. Aunt Ben stood beside him with a roll of bandages, not crying, as many of the women were, but wearing such an expression of divine pity as made her homely features almost beautiful. Eleanor, who had silently made her way to my side, wore also a calm face, but trem-

bled excessively. Suddenly the man with
whom I had already spoken observed coolly,
'Your Cousin Cecil digs well, sir ; don't he?
He's been longer in than any of 'em, and the
barrow still comes out as quick as ever.'

'Is Cecil in the pit?' asked I in wonder
not unmixed with alarm.

'Yes, surely. He came up just as the
third turn was called, and dashed in with
the spade like a good un. He's used to
the work, it seems ; but he must be nearly
spent by this time.'

'What a noble fellow !' ejaculated a
sweet, low voice behind me. I turned,
and saw Lady Repton : the tenderness of
her woman's heart made her fair face wo-
ful, and showed its lines, but I liked it
better so than I had ever done before.

'Fred would dig too, if he knew how,'
said Eleanor, taking, I suppose, her ladyship's observation as a reflection upon my
own inactivity, which I am sure it was not
intended to be.

'Yes,' said I, 'I would do so willingly, but I should be a hindrance rather than a help; whereas Cecil—'

Here I stopped abruptly. To tell how Cecil had learned to use the spade, would have been at once to disclose, at least to one of those two, the motive that was now giving such unwonted vigour to his arm. As I thought of that, I looked round for Jane, but she was nowhere to be seen. I felt glad of this, on all accounts, but in the first place, because she would naturally have been much alarmed at her brother's perilous position; for there *was* very considerable peril in it. The spadesman in such cases was, of course, the most advanced of the workers; for though, as he dug, it was the duty of the propper to make all safe behind him, he was by no means unlikely to be caught by a new fall of sand; and especially would this be the case if his anxiety to effect a rescue should make him incautious; and was Cecil likely

to be prudent, digging as he was for something that, in his eyes, was dearer far than
buried treasure in those of a miser? Every
breath that was now lent to him might eke
out the scanty stock of it in his beloved
Ruth; for the theory of the poor girl's
position, based on the firm ground of experience, was this, that if alive at all, if
not hopelessly crushed and smothered, she
must be in some confined spot, the air of
which must needs be speedily exhausted.
She had certainly not been killed outright
by the first fall—I say first, because there
were generally more than one in such cases
—since the little boy had heard a muffled
cry of 'Help!' from her after the pit had
caved in.   Perhaps, even now, that cry was
ringing in poor Cecil's ears within there!
It could not do so much longer, that was
certain.   I saw old Mr. Bourne take out
his great silver watch, ask some question of
his son—doubtless as to the time the accident had happened—and then shake his

head despondingly: this was followed by a sorrowful murmur from the crowd, as though that expression of the old man's opinion had found an audible echo.

Suddenly a voice was heard within the pit, and every eye began to twinkle with anxiety, every head to crane forward.

'Back, back!' cried my father in authoritative tones; 'leave plenty of space round the pit's mouth.' As the crowd mechanically obeyed him, the barrow-man came running out without his customary load. 'They are coming!' he exclaimed, then took his place in the mass of onlookers.

No one asked *who* were coming; but a party in the back-ground, who had been engaged in forming a couple of litters, or it might be biers, out of fir-poles, now came forward with them; while the blankets were spread out ready for instant use. It was an awful moment: dear Eleanor stole her trembling arm in mine, as if for support: and Lady Repton placed her little hand upon a pitman's shoulder. If a thunderbolt had fallen on the terrace, it would scarcely, I verily believe, have at that moment drawn away our gaze from the cave-mouth, on which all eyes were riveted. The propman had already made his appearance; and now came Cecil, tottering under the weight of a burden scarce more ghastly than himself—the corpse, as it seemed, of beautiful Ruth Waller. Her face, like his, was white and damp; her long black hair trailed over her shoulders, and mixed with his, and both were clotted with sand. But while his limbs shook beneath him, hers hung down limp and lifeless; and while his laboured breathing could be heard by the most distant spectator, Rue did not seem to breathe at all.

'Next turn!' cried old Mr. Bourne, and instantly the work within the cave commenced again; but for my part I had neither eyes nor ears except for Cecil and Ruth. The thought that Richard Waller had brought this misery on his innocent sister, steeled my heart against him, even in that bitter hour—for which I had afterwards cause for shame.

Ruth was set down on the blankets; and my father knelt down on one side of her, and Aunt Ben on the other, while Cecil, kneeling at her feet, gazed at her shut white face with unspeakable tenderness and agony.

'Hush!' You could hear the woodpigeon's murmur in the distant firs, and the flow of the far-off river, as my father leaned down his ear and listened for her breathing.

'She lives!' said he, looking up to us with tender gravity.

'Thank God!' ejaculated the rector solemnly.

I am sure that most of us did thank Him. It would have indeed been hard if cruel Death had snatched so fair a form, and laid it in the grave for a bridal bed.

But though not dead, Ruth was quite insensible, or, rather, she knew nothing of what was happening about her, for suddenly she cried out, 'A spade, a spade!' doubtless filled with some vague sense of the fate she had so narrowly escaped. It was, of course, not to be thought of that she should be taken to her own cottage, that would presently receive for its only other inmate the dead body of her brother (for although the pitmen in no way relaxed their efforts to save him, we all felt that *his* case was hopeless); and I saw Aunt Ben whisper to my father, who threw a troubled look towards Cecil. She had doubtless proposed that the poor girl should be taken to the Manor-house.

'The Rectory is nearer,' suggested Nelly boldly, yet without venturing to glance in the direction of her grandfather, whose countenance at this proposition began to evince stronger feeling than it had yet shown throughout the whole affair. He was understood to murmur something about the spare bed not being aired.

'She shall have *my* bed,' said Nelly; and with that poor Ruth, who had already been laid upon the litter, was about to be borne away.

'Stop!' cried Cecil, speaking for the first time, and laying his hand on the shoulder of the nearest bearer. 'That is my place, if you please;' and the man gave way, and he took his place accordingly.

I can see the whole scene now, as though it were before my very eyes—Cecil's grave quickness, and the bearer's stolid wonder; my father's pained surprise, and the amaze and interest of all the rest, so great, that, in spite of the tragedy that was simultaneously taking place, it expressed itself in murmurs; then the little procession slowly moving off with even pace along the noiseless sand, and Eleanor walking by Ruth Waller's side with her cold hand in hers.

CHAPTER X.

Not till an hour had elapsed after Ruth's rescue, was her unhappy brother brought forth from the pit that had been his grave. It was evident, from the appearance of the body, that he had long been a dead man, and we all hoped that the fall which had overwhelmed him had slain him on the spot. This, however, as it turned out, had not been the case. In a day or two, Ruth was sufficiently recovered to narrate the circumstances of the catastrophe, and they were such as amazed and shocked our little community, even more than the event itself.

When her brother and herself went to work as usual on that morning, they had found that, except from a few yards of passage at the entrance, the whole of the props supporting the roof had been removed. The idea that Richard himself had made away with them for the purpose of supplying himself with the means of purchasing drink, was one that had not even occurred to his sister; nor was it afterwards ever suggested to her, since the fact itself seemed abundantly disproved by her evidence, corroborated as it was by that of the little boy, her assistant. Richard Waller had expressed himself with too much vehemence and indignation against the author of the heartless theft, to be suspected of being himself the culprit: his nature was anything but hypocritical; it was, on the contrary, rash and impulsive, as was fatally evidenced by his conduct on the occasion in question; which at the same time convinced us that we had done him wrong in attributing to him a selfish disregard of his sister's safety. 'Prop or no prop,' he had passionately exclaimed, 'I do my work to-day as usual; and if anything happens to me, my blood be on the villain's head that has done this thing! But as for thee, lass,' he had added, ' keep thou within the props, with the boy.'

In vain Ruth had endeavoured to combat this rash resolve. Early as it was, the unhappy man had already partaken of strong liquor, and was in no condition to be argued with, while the theft of the props had excited him beyond control. All that his poor sister could do was to keep as near to him as possible, in order to give him warning of impending peril, though her doing so angered him exceedingly, and more than once he had driven her back with words that she now trembled to recall. ' If Mr. Cecil had only been with me, *as usual*,' the poor half-conscious girl had pitifully complained to Nelly (and by that phrase had told her all), ' he would have compelled Richard to take heed.' She had taken great care, however, to keep the child well

within the covered gallery, and given him
instructions as to what to do in case of any
mischance; which he afterwards most fortunately carried out with promptitude. When
the accident occurred, she had her back towards her brother, and was carrying away
a basket of sand—poor Rue never used the
barrow, because the handling of it spoiled
her hands—for the boy to take without,
and empty; and the sudden extinction of
her brother's candle was the first indication
she received of what had happened. Immediately afterwards a dull 'thud,' as she expressed it, rang in her ears, and she was
herself knocked down by the descent of the
sand. In neither case, as it seemed, had
the sides given way (as is most usual in
such calamities), but a portion of the roof
itself had fallen in block; the mass that
had buried Ruth was partly supported by
the basket of sand, beside which she lay;
and to its scanty protection she doubtless
owed her preservation. Though much

bruised by the blow, and greatly oppressed by the superincumbent weight, she did not lose consciousness, and could distinctly hear her brother's pitiful moans. The sand had fallen on him in a wedge-shaped mass, and thereby protracted his sufferings for a brief interval, by allowing him space wherein to breathe. She was so near to him, notwithstanding the dense barrier between them, that she could even overhear him call to her in muffled tones, and utter the fragments of a prayer. Prone on the damp earth, in total darkness, and with the expectation of instant death, the sound of his voice, she said, shot to her a ray of comfort. She had endeavoured to reply to him, but the sand choked her, while the effort to speak gave her intense pain. 'I am a murdered man,' she heard him say; and then there was a second and greater fall of earth, 'as though the whole cliff had come down upon him.' Then all was silent as the grave.

After what seemed an eternity of time, she heard the strokes of the pick and spade; but these, though in reality approaching her, appeared to grow duller and duller, and presently altogether ceased. She had, in fact, become unconscious, and was probably on the very threshold of death, when Cecil's pickaxe let in the air, and revived her. She did not know even now that it was he who had rescued her, nor did she speak of him at all, with the single exception I have mentioned. Her whole thoughts seemed to be fixed on her dead brother, upon the cause of whose sad fate she was incessantly speculating. He had not had an enemy in the world, so far as she knew, and yet she did not need his dying words to be convinced that the theft of the props had been committed of *malice prepense;* that whoever had stolen them counted on his well-known imprudence inducing him to work on as usual, and had thereby compassed his death. What con-

firmed this view of the case with us all (in
spite of our unwillingness to adopt so harsh
a theory) was, that the stolen props themselves were discovered in an open space of
the wood above the cave, so that they had
certainly not been taken for the sake of the
few shillings they would have fetched in
the 'pit' market.

This important question greatly occu-
pied all minds, especially those of the local
magistracy, of which old Mr. Bourne and
my father were both members. The latter,
as I well knew (though he kept silence on
the subject), was also full of anxious thought
concerning Cecil, whose conduct since the
catastrophe was even more significant with
respect to Ruth than it had been on the
occasion of her rescue. He called at the
Rectory twice a day, to inquire how she
was progressing; and scoured the country
round, in the character of an amateur de-
tective, in hopes to gain some clue that
might lead to the discovery of the culprit.

Curiously enough, not a word of remonstrance passed his sister's lips, though she
could not but have been aware of his proceedings. Perhaps she was rather more re-
served and morose in manner than before;
but that might have arisen from physical
causes, since her indisposition still continued,
though not so severely as to confine her to
her own room. No one liked to speak of
recent events in her presence, because of
the share her brother had had in them;
and yet we could think of little else. Our
theatricals had been put an end to because
of them, for Cecil had declined to act; and
the gaiety of our little party was utterly
quenched. Lord and Lady Repton took
their departure on the very day that was
to have been witness to the entertainment
of the county at the Theatre Royal, Gatcombe; and her ladyship, I verily believe,
was more disappointed at the withdrawal
of the piece than was its author himself.
For my part, my apprehensions upon Cecil's

account swallowed up all minor causes of melancholy: the present distress was, I felt only too well convinced, but the prelude to some grave occurrence which was likely to throw no temporary shadow on our home-life. The preparations for the inquest at present gave my father an excuse for silence; he was probably averse to speak to Cecil while the latter was so full of excitement (for Ruth herself was still in a somewhat critical condition); but it was impossible that the *éclaircissement* could be long deferred. What the end of it all would be, it was difficult to guess; but the affair looked gloomy from every point of view for all of us; while as for me, I was only too sensible that any knowledge of Cecil's headstrong attachment was taken for granted, and that for the first time in my life I had grievously displeased my father.

The coroner's inquest took place at Holksham, a small town half way to Monkton, where the magistrates' meeting was

wont to be held once a fortnight; and the
finding was one which, if not legally justi-
fied by the fact, was still only what might
have been expected from the heated state
of the public mind, greatly aggravated as
it was by the excited testimony of Ruth
herself. The jury adopted her unfortunate
brother's last words, and returned a verdict
of 'Wilful murder against some person or
persons unknown.' My father was not present; but Cecil and I had attended throughout the proceedings, and the former evinced
great satisfaction at the result of the inquiry. 'If ever there was a man who de-
served hanging,' observed he in the drawing-room that evening, with a vehemence
that was quite unusual with him, 'it was
the man who brought the cliff down upon
poor Richard Waller.' My father quietly
combated this opinion. He allowed, of
course, that if there had been any intention
to do him hurt, the crime was of the deep-
est dye; but if the props had been merely

stolen to make money of them, and considering that nine men out of ten would
have desisted from work upon discovery of
their loss, he thought the offence could not
be stretched so far. We all listened to this
controversy in embarrassed silence; for we
knew what underlay the feelings of both
disputants, and had an uneasy apprehension
that Ruth's name might presently be mentioned by one of them. Cecil was greatly
excited; and, indeed, if that had not been
the case, he would not have contended with
my father at all, whom he always treated
with a respect approaching to reverence.
Aunt Ben's fingers trembled so excessively,
that she laid down her knitting, and took
up a certain *History of the Drama* which
had been given to her by Lady Repton.
She had religiously tried to get through it
during her ladyship's stay; but Cecil had
mischievously put back her book-marker
daily, so that she always began at the fif-
teenth page or so, and unconsciously went

over the same ground; but on this occasion
she did not progress even so much as usual,
for she held the volume upside down. Cousin Jane was apparently devoted to her Chinese puzzle; but I noticed that the same
piece was retained in her hand, and never
put down, with such rapt attention was she
listening to what was being said.

'If Richard Waller had not an enemy
in the world, my dear Cecil,' continued my
father, 'the *malice prepense* which consti-
tutes "murder" could not have existed. The
verdict, therefore, is evidently incorrect and
strained.'

'But he might have had an enemy without knowing it,' argued Cecil: 'there have
been cases of that kind before now.'

'That is true,' said my father gravely;
'some men have their worst enemies in
those that seem to be dearest to them.'

At this, Aunt Ben's book dropped out
of her hand. (She afterwards told me it
made her so 'all of a pug,' that, if she had

had her knitting-needles, they would certainly have been rusted.) Most happily, however, as it appeared to us all, Cecil did not reply. The discussion seemed over for that evening. My father took up Ben Jonson; and Cecil went to the piano, and 'picked out' a tune. He was not so good a performer on that instrument as on the flute, but he played fairly and with feeling. After a little, he struck into his favourite melody, 'And ye shall walk in silk attire.' It was curious that he should have chosen it on that occasion, since the moral of the piece in question is certainly opposed to unequal marriages; but perhaps it recommended itself to him on that very account, just as a man who is quite certain of his own logical position is not averse to quote the arguments of his opponents.

In the middle of it, my father laid down his book, and suddenly exclaimed: 'Cecil, I want to speak to you.'

My cousin stopped his tune at once, but

remained sitting on the music-stool; while my father stood up, with his back to the mantelpiece. We all knew what was coming.

'I had intended, my dear boy, to have our talk out to-night in private, in my study; but, upon second thoughts, I think it better to address you in the presence of those who love you, and whom you love, that they may add their entreaties—if entreaties should be necessary—to mine. I need hardly waste time in asking you, Cecil, what has unhappily been made of late so abundantly manifest, whether it is true that you have formed a serious attachment to Ruth Waller; and yet I will not take it for granted. Is it true?'

'It is quite true, sir,' returned Cecil firmly, and looking fixedly in my father's face.

'May I ask how long this has been the case? for it has been kept from me altogether until within these few days'—

here my father turned a reproachful glance on me — 'a want of confidence which I should not have expected.'

'I beseech you, sir, do not be angry with Fred,' pleaded Cecil earnestly : 'he has only been silent for your sake. He would have told you all, months ago, but for my threat that, if he did so, I would marry Ruth at once, as I most surely would have done. It is I alone who am to blame; not he, nor Ruth.'

Here he looked towards his sister half defiantly; and I fully expected to hear her make some contemptuous reply; but she kept silence, her devotion to her puzzle becoming more assiduous than ever.

'Do I understand you to mean, Cecil, continued my father very gravely, 'that it is your final resolve to marry this girl?— One moment before you answer. Let me premise that I have no authority over you whatsoever, by your father's will, the use of which could prevent your putting such a scheme into practice; I have no menace to employ of any sort. You are your own master, except as regards money matters; and even in that respect I shall exercise no power to your disadvantage.'

I saw Aunt Ben give a glance of remonstrance at my father; and Jane's forehead darken, as she bent lower over her little table; while, on the other hand, Cecil's resolute expression softened—it was still decisive; but the decision was mingled with tenderness.

'You are far too sensible,' continued my father, 'and I will say also, notwithstanding what you now propose, far too unselfish, not to have set before yourself some of the consequences that must ensue to others in case of your committing this act of—well—imprudence. But I think some have escaped your attention. It has been the endeavour of your aunt and myself to make you feel this house to be your home.'

'It has—it has, indeed, sir,' interrupted Cecil gently. 'I have felt it deeply.'

'I am sure you have, my dear lad; but it has not struck you that it can never be the home of Ruth Waller. It has not occurred to you, that in marrying her you will not only give up your *own* position in society—not a great sacrifice, you will say, perhaps: well, you will not think so ten years hence; but it is not worth while to argue that matter—but also that of your sister. I say nothing of the pain and distress that such an alliance must needs cause to my own little household. I am not a man to attach undue importance to birth and station; but I confess—' Here he stopped, and pointed significantly to poor Aunt Ben, who was dissolved in tears. 'We shall get over it in time, you think; and perhaps we shall; at all events, we are old; and it is only natural, doubtless, that what concerns your whole future life should have more weight with you than considerations

for what may seem to you our temporary
convenience. But Jane, remember, is no
older than yourself; and let me tell you,
that you will be putting her in a most disadvantageous position, as respects her prospects, by allying yourself to this girl. Do
not imagine, my dear lad, that I am under-
rating your temptation. It has well been
said, that

" The treasures of the deep are not so precious
    As are the concealed comforts of a man
    Locked up in woman's love."

I use no arguments about thoughtless passion and love's quick satiety, because you
will only smile at them. It seems to you,
I know, that Beauty will keep her lustrous
eyes, and Young Love pine after them for
ever; but I appeal to the very heart from
which that love (if it be worth anything)
upsprings. Do not sacrifice your sister's
prospects for the gratification—I do not
say of your own happiness, for you will not

be happy, my poor lad—but of your present pleasure.'

'How do I sacrifice my sister's prospects, uncle?' inquired Cecil quietly.

'In this way, my boy. All young women naturally look forward to the time when they shall have a home of their own —in other words, to marriage. Jane is not an heiress independent of circumstances; and the fact of your having made an ignoble alliance would without doubt greatly prejudice her future.'

'I see,' replied Cecil softly.—'Heaven forbid that any act of mine should harm you, Jane!' and here he glanced towards his sister lovingly. 'As regards fortune, since our dear uncle has alluded to it, I may tell you that it both was and is my intention to do away, so far as I have power to do so, with the inequality between us in that respect.'

He stopped a moment; and for the first time Cousin Jane looked up, and, with a

faint smile, seemed to acknowledge his ge-
nerosity; then shot a glance towards me,
to the meaning of which, thanks to Lady
Repton, I could not be blind: 'I shall be
rich, you hear,' it seemed to say.

'Every one that knows you, Cecil,'
struck in my father with tenderness (and
indeed it is impossible that his manner
throughout could have been more carefully
framed to conciliate, and not to wound),
'will credit you with generous impulses;
but, in the first place, it will not be so easy
to do for your sister as you propose, effec-
tually; and secondly, there will still re-
main the fact, that you, her brother, have
married a labourer's daughter, a labourer's
sister, a girl with low connections—'

'Pardon me, uncle,' interrupted Cecil;
'Ruth has no relative, that can be called
such, *now*. A few days ago, I allow, your
argument would have had more force. I
was not unconscious, as Fred will tell you
—indeed, I felt most acutely—that Richard

Waller—was a—a grievous obstacle, in short, to my own selfish views; though, Heaven knows, I wished him no harm; he is dead, poor fellow! and that obstacle has been removed.' He stopped again, and in the silence we heard the front-door bell violently ring. 'As for Ruth herself, sir, you do not know her; she is not the dull village girl that you imagine her to be. Perhaps a day will come when you will not only confess as much, but even not be ashamed to receive her, as others will, I am persuaded, as my wife, and as a true lady, though not so by birth. Lady Repton, as I have heard, sir, was not born a lady.'

'My dear lad,' said my father, 'these are dreams.'

'Still, I live in them, and cannot live without them,' answered Cecil softly, and yet with a certain dignity, that to me at least seemed very touching. 'I am most grieved to oppose myself to you, whom I respect and honour, and whom I would lay down my life to serve; but Ruth is dearer to me than my life.'

His fingers, which still rested on the keys, seemed mechanically to produce the last verse of the song he had been playing:

'And ere I'm found to break my faith,
I'll lay me down and dee.' ,

My father looked very grave, and was about again to speak, when the door opened, and the parlour-maid entered hurriedly.

'O sir, please, sir,' said she nervously, 'there's somebody wants to see you.'

'I can see nobody just now,' was my father's stern rejoinder; indeed, I had never heard him speak so harshly, his manner to all his servants being always gentle in the extreme.

'But, please, sir, it's most particular,' urged the girl, frightened by her master's manner, but still more frightened, as it seemed, by the intelligence she had to communicate.

' Let him come to-morrow morning; or, if you know his business, state it.'

'Well, sir—O dear! O dear!—it's the parish constable, and he's been and found the murderer!'

We jumped up from our seats—all, that is, save one of us: Cousin Jane fell back in hers with a sharp shrill cry, and fainted away.

CHAPTER XI.

I⊤ is one of the disadvantages of being stu-
diously reticent and undemonstrative, that
when the feelings *do* get the better of such
persons, they are apt to exhibit themselves
in some abnormal condition far more unpleasant and astonishing than are the usual
tokens of surprise or woe. A man who
never shares a grief becomes dyspeptic, and
goes mad; a woman who never sheds a tear,
has fits; and thus it happened to Cousin
Jane, though it was only a fainting-fit. Not
a word had she spoken throughout that
discussion between my father and Cecil,
notwithstanding that she herself had partly
formed the subject of it, and had even been
indirectly appealed to. Not a sign had she

given of interest in the man whose terrible
fate had precipitated the discovery of Cecil's
' love affair.' She had hidden every trace
of feeling, save that in place of working as
usual at the Chinese puzzle, she had stuck
in the middle of it, like an automaton chess-
player out of repair; and thus, when the
news that Martha brought, ' He's been and
found the murderer,' fell suddenly on her
ear, her nerves, unnaturally braced, had
fairly given way, and total prostration followed. I saw her face, as Cecil leaped to
her aid, and anything more ghastly it was
impossible to imagine. If the parlour-maid
had opened the door with, ' Please, sir, the
murderer,' and introduced some gentleman
dripping with gore, the sensation, so far as
Cousin Jane was concerned, could not have
been more complete or stupendous. She
was carried up, unconscious, to her room;
and the shock, acting, doubtless, on a sys-
tem enfeebled by recent indisposition, affected her very seriously. We did not see

her again for days. Aunt Ben, on the other
hand, impressionable and sympathetic by
nature with respect to all 'her own belong-
ings,' as she called them, and by no means
philosophic even as regarded human affairs
in general, bore Martha's piece of news with
reasonable composure, though she admitted
that the communication of it had 'given
her a turn.' It was, however, the circumstances under which the news had arrived,
perhaps—late at night, and when our minds
were curiously enough engaged on a subject so closely connected with it—rather
than the news itself that was startling, or
even strange. That the man who had removed the props from the sand-pit should,
sooner or later, be found out, was only what
might have been expected; and now that
he *was* found, he had not even the ordinary
attraction of a detected villain, for it was
only poor half-witted 'Batty' after all.

As the village idiot had already been
convicted of a similar offence, it might na-

turally have been supposed that all eyes
would at once have turned upon him with
suspicion in the present instance ; but this
had not been the case. That some had
charged him with the crime, was true ; but
he had denied the fact with a characteristic
irritation that seemed to have the force of
truth, and his simple, inoffensive nature
had been too well understood for him to
become the object of general suspicion.   If
the props had been taken for gain, it would
have been another matter; but poor Batty
was certainly not the man to have removed
the props for mere mischief, even though
he might not have realised to himself the
peril of such a proceeding.   There was another reason, too, why he should have
escaped, at all events, the scrutiny of the
coroner's inquest, in the absence of any po-
sitive proof of his guilt : it was commonly
believed that he was a natural son of old
Mr. Bourne.   The Alchemist's reputation
was by no means unsullied as a man of

gallantry, though he did not look like a
Belmour or a Lothario.   Though so emi-
nently sagacious (after his fashion), he was,
in fact, credited with a weakness for the
fair sex up to rather an advanced period
of life ; with being very 'human,' if not
'humane ;' and I fear that village scandal
did not in this matter do him wrong.
At all events, since this great man had
chosen in his wisdom to utterly neglect
Batty from the cradle (or whatever had
been his cheap substitute for that commo-
dity), it was obviously not for his depend-
ents, the village folk, to bring the poor
fellow into prominence on the present occasion.   After his denial, therefore, of the offence in question, which had besides been
never laid seriously to his charge, Batty had
been left unmolested, and, perhaps, would
not have been farther troubled about it, but
for his own act. When the verdict of Wilful
Murder, however, was being discussed in
the village alehouse in his presence, a sense

of the importance which would accrue to the culprit seemed to strike him forcibly, and he had made frank and full confession.

'I took the props away,' said the poor creature; 'and now I shall be taken to London town and hanged;' an idea that evidently gave him the greatest satisfaction. He would see the metropolis (as he erroneously imagined), at all events, and would probably become a great public character, which—locally—he undoubtedly did. The village constable had, on his part, taken him up, with as deep a conviction of the greatness of his charge, as the official who conveyed the seven bishops to the Tower could possibly have experienced; and had then come down to the Manor-house, as I have said, to report his exploit—to mention himself, as it were, conspicuously, in his own despatches.

Except upon Mr. Bourne's account, it was clearly a matter of congratulation that the offence was thus brought home to one

to whom it could certainly not be imputed
as a crime; and my father, who was a man
who shut his ears to all scandals, had, at
first, not even that alloy to his satisfaction.
But on that very night, late as it was, the
Alchemist made his appearance, and was
closeted with him in the study for more
than an hour, a fact which raised many
eyebrows and loosened many tongues. It
was remembered that on the last occasion
of Batty's getting into trouble, it was Mr.
Bourne, from his place on the magistrates'
bench, who had pooh-poohed the inquiry;
and, though generally a harsh administrator
of justice, had caused the prisoner to be
dismissed with a light reprimand; and the
purpose of his present untimely visit was
unhesitatingly set down to his wish to induce my father to 'burke' inquiry into the
present business. It was even reported that
he had offered to restore the Manor lands
to the House of Wray, if he would cause
the matter to be hushed up—a proposition

most unlikely to be made by such a man, and one which, if made, would undoubtedly have resulted in his being instantly turned out of the house. He would, indeed, I am persuaded, as soon have dared to ask Aunt Ben's virgin hand in marriage. Certain it is, however, that what he did say turned my father's contempt for the old man into disgust. His age had hitherto protected him from his satire, which subsequently it failed to do; and never shall I forget, when, some time afterwards, the old fellow was chuckling over his acquisition of some gain in stock or share like a male witch, the form which my father's congratulation took. ' You are fortunate still,' said he, in the words of Middleton :

> ' The very screech-owl lights upon your shoulder,
> And woos you like a pigeon.'

The result of the interview was, in the end, not without its bearing upon my own fortunes, when it came to Mr. Bourne's turn to influence them; but, for the present, it ended in the complete discomfiture of that worthy.

The ensuing day happened to be that appointed for one of the fortnightly magistrates' meetings at Holksham, and at it Batty was arraigned accordingly before a bench of three. Both Cecil and myself accompanied my father, and were 'accommodated with seats' on that imaginary elevation—for, as a matter of fact, each justice had a wooden chair—while the little court-house was crammed to the utmost by all Gatcombe. On account of the locality wherein the offence had been committed, my father was not, as usual, elected chairman (a most fortunate circumstance, as it afterwards turned out) ; and the same reason disqualifying Mr. Bourne, the dignity was conferred on Mr. Close, Frank's father ; an excellent divine, but one not altogether adapted by nature for the performance of magisterial functions. He was very deaf, and very fussy ; and if the degrees of human

intelligence should be expressed by the ten
digits, progressively, that of the Rev. F. Close,
J.P., would have been represented by the
figure 2, at highest. Poor Batty's, however,
stood only at $\frac{1}{2}$ or so, and he quailed before
that important and awe-inspiring man as a
mouse before an owl. Weeping and wring-
ing his hands, he pitifully expressed his
contrition for his offence even before it had
been formally laid to his charge; while,
dividing the public attention with him, old
Mr. Bourne, on the seat remotest from our
little party, drooped his shaggy eyebrows
and bit his nails. It may be imagined,
therefore, that the whole scene contained
elements of dramatic interest, and for my
part I could not help reflecting how excel-
lently it might be adapted for the stage.

'Hum, ha!' said the chairman, regarding Batty with a solemn shake of his white
head. 'What is the prisoner's name, policeman?'

Now, this question, simple as it seemed,

was not an easy one for anybody to answer,
and totally beyond the power of the person
interrogated.

'Well, your worship, it's just "Batty,"'
returned the constable, in hesitating accents;
and indeed the poor fellow had never been
known, save in the parish register, where,
I suppose, he had been entered under his
matronymic, by any other name. Everybody looked at old Mr. Bourne, and one or
two (far back in the crowd) even began to
snigger.

'Hum, ha!' reiterated the chairman, his
face and bald head becoming red as a new-
born infant with the sudden recollection of
the *scandalum magnatum* against his bro-
ther-magistrate. 'Very good; proceed with
the charge.' Whereupon Batty having
pleaded 'Not guilty,' the village constable
had his innings, and detailed the circumstances of the prisoner's capture and confession with painstaking circumlocution,
and reiterated expressions of hope that his

evidence might give pleasure to their worships.

'Are you sure now, policeman,' inquired the chairman sternly, 'that this acknowledgment of the prisoner's guilt that you have detailed to us was made of his own free-will, and after due warning had been given to him, that whatever he said might subsequently be used against him?'

'Lor bless your worship,' replied the constable, looking towards Batty with a pitying smile, 'he couldn't have understood nothin' o' that—not he.'

'I don't ask you whether the prisoner would have understood you, sir,' exclaimed the chairman irascibly; 'I ask whether you gave him due legal admonishment?'

Mr. Bourne nodded approval in reply to the sweeping glance of triumph at his own sagacity that here emanated from the Chair, and a murmur of applause arose from the spectators.

'Justice Close knows how to tackle a

fellow, mind ye, when it comes to law,' was an opinion uttered in my hearing, and received with marks of general adhesion. The constable's air, of late so impressively suggestive of having done his country a good turn, now became quite chop-fallen.

'Well, no, your worship; I can't say as I did.'

'Did what, sir?' inquired the inexorable chairman. 'Let us hear the whole truth.'

'Well, I didn't give him no due—whatever your worship pleased to call it—my old woman and me, we only gave him his supper.'

A roar of laughter followed this announcement, in which poor Batty joined tumultuously. He thought that everything was now good-humouredly arranged, and made an attempt to get out of his box, which had to be frustrated by physical force.

'It seems to me, Mr. Chairman,' observed Mr. Bourne, in a husky voice, 'that

the evidence we have just heard, having
been illegally extracted by the constable,
on the prisoner's own confession, is quite
worthless, and cannot be used against the
accused at all.'

'What, what? Then what the deuce
is to be done?' returned the chairman in
a whisper. 'Can't dismiss the case, you
know; that's impossible.'

'Why not?' answered the old man in
the same low tones; 'there's no case to go
on with.'

'No case! Why, I'm come here on
purpose; pooh, pooh.—What do *you* say,
Mr. Wray?'

My father shrugged his shoulders: he
knew well enough what should be done, I
saw, but he did not wish to take any lead-
ing part in the affair. 'Ask the clerk,' said
he curtly.

Now the magistrates' clerk at Holksham
(as in one or two other country seats of
justice in these isles) was in fact the sole

authority from which all judgments of the bench were derived; but the fiction was always kept up among the Great Unpaid of his being the mere amanuensis and recorder of their legal decisions. To 'ask the clerk' was therefore an impossible suggestion, and one which caused the Rev. Mr. Close to frown and shake his head; but he bent down over the table, and held a consultation with that functionary in a low tone, the peculiarity of which was that all the signs of gesture-language were reversed in it, so that to the eyes of the spectators it appeared as if the clerk were humbly putting his interrogatories, and the chairman blandly but firmly laying down the law. It was really a very clever performance on the part of his worship, and got him great credit; but it was even a still cleverer on the part of the clerk, since it got him not only credit, but insured the continuance of a salary of some hundreds a year.

'Let those witnesses be summoned,' observed the chairman, speaking aloud, and with great dignity, ' upon whose information the constable was induced to arrest the prisoner.'

At this there was a slight commotion in the crowd, as though two or three persons were making a hurried exit; and when the constable had indicated who the proposed witnesses were, it was discovered that they were not in court; for to be connected with a great public event in its first stage—such as picking up a man who has been run over by a Hansom-cab, or running for the fire-escape when we see flames—is often very gratifying; whereas some subsequent development of the affair—such as an inquest, or an action at law by an insurance company—may cause us a good deal of trouble, if it does not seriously compromise us.

Thus, in the skittle-ground of the Red Lion, it had doubtless been very pleasant to detect a wilful murderer; but it was not at all pleasant to have to prove the fact on oath before the Holksham bench, and then to be 'bound over,' perhaps, to do it again before the still more impressive majesty of the judges of assize. The constable's self-important airs had persuaded his informers that all responsibility had been shifted to his official shoulders, and now that they found themselves about to share it, they had turned and fled. The getting up of criminal cases, as may be inferred, was not an art brought to perfection at Holksham.

The witnesses having in vain been summoned, the proceedings came once more to a dead-lock; and again Mr. Bourne remonstrated with 'the chair' against the case being proceeded with.

'But we are not proceeding, Mr. Bourne,' argued the unhappy chairman; 'we are waiting for evidence.'

'You may do as you please, Mr. Chairman,' answered the old man, raising his voice, 'but it will be at your own risk. I am not at all sure that the prisoner may not have grounds for bringing an action against us for false imprisonment. He has pleaded "Not guilty," and nothing has been brought forward—'

'Please, your worships,' here exclaimed one of the constables in charge of Batty, 'the prisoner is a-telling us as how he did it.'

'What do you mean?' ejaculated the chairman incredulously, yet welcoming any solution of the difficulty in which he found himself involved. 'He's not saying he is guilty, is he?'

'I did it, I did it!' here broke out poor Batty, wearied with the tediousness of the proceedings, and thoroughly disenchanted of the attractions of a public position. 'I stole the props, and made the cave fall in. There, there! Now let's be off to London.'

It was a pitiful sight to behold the witless, friendless lad (he was not much over twenty, and looked younger) turning from one to the other of those who stood about him, and pleading to be taken away. Even old Mr. Bourne had for once the sympathies of his hearers with him, when he pointed out to the chairman the absurdity of pursuing so serious a charge against one who had manifestly shown himself an irresponsible agent.

'But there's a man been killed,' urged Mr. Close; 'and here's the fellow that did it, and *says* he did it.'

'That's just the point, my good sir. This unfortunate lad will say anything, because, as everybody is aware, he does not know what he says.'

'Well, well, you know more about him than I do, Mr. Bourne: that is,' stammered thé chairman, 'you ought to do so; I mean, because he belongs to your parish. But we who sit here have nothing to do with previous acquaintance with an accused person—What do *you* say, Mr. Wray?'

'If you ask my opinion,' said my father gravely, 'I must needs say that, since we have this poor fellow before us protesting that he committed the offence with which he is charged, I see no other alternative than to send him for trial. A judge and a jury are as competent to perceive his irresponsibility as ourselves. Indeed, we have no power, as it seems to me, to deal with the matter otherwise.'

The chairman looked towards the clerk, who, with obsequious face, seemed to reply: 'Just as you please, sir; you are the best judge;' but I caught in his deferential whisper the words: 'Your only course,' and 'the Home Secretary;' and then Mr. Close's answer: 'The devil it is: then that settles it.'

Then the chairman blew his nose, like a trumpeter proclaiming silence, settled his spectacles, that had been disturbed by that operation, and addressed Batty in solemn tones.

'Prisoner at the bar, you stand committed.'

'I didn't commit it,' roared Batty; 'I was set on to do it. I was given money to do it.'

'Set on to do it! money!' ejaculated Mr. Close.

'Yes, money,' repeated Batty in a grudging tone. 'I knew I shouldn't be allowed to keep it—I never am; I have got it in the waistband of my breeches. They've taken away my knife, or I would let you see the gold.'

'He *has* got money, your worship,' said the constable, rapidly investigating the repository thus indicated, 'though I'm sure I searched him through and through. Here are five golden sovereigns.'

If Batty had suddenly announced himself in possession of his five wits, and had laid them for inspection on the magistrates' table, they could not have excited greater wonderment than did the exhibition of this wealth. That Batty should have been in possession of such a sum was indeed as astonishing as though a vein of gold should have suddenly been come upon in the sand-cliff; a few shillings was the very most the poor fellow had ever had to call his own in his life; indeed, as a general rule, he did not earn sufficient to support himself, his scanty wages being supplemented by charity and parish relief.

'Where did you get this gold from, Batty?' said my father gravely; his magisterial functions utterly lost sight of for the moment, in the interest which this unexpected turn had given to the case. If this poor lad had really been bribed to remove the props, there was murder in the matter with a vengeance; but of course it seemed more probable that he had stolen the gold. That was the view, also, which even Batty understood his audience to entertain, for he replied at once: 'It's my own money; it was given me for taking away the props.'

'Good heavens!' ejaculated Cecil in my ear. 'Did you ever hear anything so horrible! Perhaps poor Richard was right, after all, when he said: "I am a murdered man." '

'When was it given to you, and by whom?' continued my father kindly. 'You will not be punished for speaking the truth, you know.'

'It was given to me last Thursday; I remember that, because I got my dinner up at the Manor-house just before. They're always good to me up there.' There was a simple gratefulness in Batty's tone that touched one, but a curious sort of apologetic hesitation also; and he cast a wistful look at his interrogator, as much as to say, 'Do you really wish me to tell?'

'It was on Thursday, was it?' said my father. 'Well, and now tell us who it was who gave you these five sovereigns to take away the props from Richard Waller's pit.'

It was a calm summer day, and though the court-house windows were all open, not a breeze was stirring; the drowsy crow of a cock alone broke the hush without, and within was unbroken silence. Every eye was fixed on Batty, and every ear was stretched to catch his answer. He hesitated, glanced nervously in our direction, and then, nodding towards my cousin, as though in unwilling recognition of him, answered simply: 'It was Mr. Cecil, yonder.'

END OF VOL. I.

LONDON:
ROBSON AND SONS, PRINTERS, PANCRAS ROAD, N.W.

December 1871.

TINSLEYS' MAGAZINE,

𝔄𝔫 𝔍𝔩𝔩𝔲𝔰𝔱𝔯𝔞𝔱𝔢𝔡 𝔐𝔬𝔫𝔱𝔥𝔩𝔶,

Price One Shilling.

Now publishing,

UNDER THE RED DRAGON. By James Grant, author of "The Romance of War," "Only an Ensign," &c.

HOME, SWEET HOME. A new Serial Story.

MUSICAL RECOLLECTIONS OF THE LAST HALF CENTURY.

The first Eight Volumes of "Tinsleys' Magazine" are now ready,
Containing :

THE MONARCH OF MINCING LANE. A complete Novel. By the Author of "The Daughter of Heth," &c.

GEORGE CANTERBURY'S WILL. A complete Novel. By Mrs. Henry Wood, author of "East Lynne," &c.

THE ROCK AHEAD. A complete Novel. By Edmund Yates, author of "Black Sheep," &c.

BREAKING A BUTTERFLY. A complete Novel. By the Author of "Guy Livingstone," &c.

AUSTIN FRIARS. A complete Novel. By Mrs. J. H. Riddell, author of "George Geith," &c.

JOSHUA MARVEL. A complete Novel. By B. L. Farjeon, author of "Grif," &c.

LADY JUDITH. A complete Novel. By Justin McCarthy, author of "My Enemy's Daughter," &c.

A HOUSE OF CARDS. A complete Novel. By Mrs. Cashel Hoey, author of "Falsely True," &c.

DOCTOR BRADY. A complete Novel. By W. H. Russell, LL.D., of the *Times.*

THE HON. ALICE BRAND'S CORRESPONDENCE.

And numerous Essays and Articles by Popular Authors.

The above Volumes are elegantly bound in cloth gilt, price 8s. per volume. Cases for Binding may be had of the Publisher, price 1s. 6d. each.

TINSLEY BROTHERS, 18 CATHERINE STREET, STRAND.

TINSLEY BROTHERS' LIST OF NEW BOOKS.

Mr. Grant's "History of the Newspaper Press."

The Newspaper Press: its Origin, Progress, and Present Position. By JAMES GRANT, author of "Random Recollections," &c. 2 vols. 8vo.

"It was natural that such a man, to whom the press had been, as it were, the atmosphere he had breathed for half a life-time, should think of recording what he personally knew, or had historically gathered, concerning that unique institution."—*Standard.*

"Alike by natural gifts, and by a life-long experience, Mr. Grant was specially qualified for being the historian of the Newspaper Press."—*Elgin Courant.*

"His experience as a writer has been considerable, and his knowledge of all matters connected with the Newspaper Press is more extensive than that of most of his contemporaries."—*Athenæum.*

"We venture, therefore, to prophesy that these two goodly volumes by Mr. Grant will be read with great interest; and as the literary banquet which the author sets before his readers is complete, *ab ovo usque ad mala*, they will be instructed and amused as well as interested."—*Notes and Queries.*

The Two Sieges. By HENRY VIZETELLY, author of "The Story of the Diamond Necklace," &c. With numerous Illustrations. 2 vols. 8vo.

Lives of the Kembles. By PERCY FITZGERALD, author of the "Life of David Garrick," &c. 2 vols. 8vo.

"Diligent and discursive. Mr. Fitzgerald has produced a clear and tolerably correct summary of all that people in general care to know about the Kembles."—*Times.*

Letters on International Relations before and during the War of 1870. By the *Times* Correspondent at Berlin. Reprinted, by permission, from the *Times*, with considerable Additions. 2 vols. 8vo. 36s.

"These letters embrace the eventful period between the respective conclusions of the two great wars to which the new German Empire owes its existence. They begin with the preliminaries of the peace of 1866; they end with the preliminaries of the peace of 1871. They resolve themselves accordingly into a history of the triumph of German unity over those jealousies and machinations that culminated in the French aggression."—*Times,* April 15.

Our Living Poets: an Essay in Criticism. By H. BUXTON FORMAN. 1 vol., 12s.

"Mr. Forman's appreciative and judicious volume of criticism will interest every reader who cares for the subject of which it treats."—*Pall Mall Gazette.*

The Idol in Horeb. Evidence that the Golden Image at Mount Sinai was a Cone and not a Calf. With Three Appendices. By CHARLES T. BEKE, Ph.D. 1 vol., 5s.

Life Beneath the Waves; and a Description of the Brighton Aquarium, with numerous Illustrations. 1 vol., 2s. 6d.

TINSLEY BROTHERS, 18 CATHERINE STREET, STRAND.

WORKS BY CAPTAIN BURTON, F.R.G.S. &c.
A New Book of Travels.

Zanzibar. By CAPTAIN R. F. BURTON, author of "A Mission to Geléle," "Explorations of the Highlands of the Brazil," "Abeokuta," "My Wanderings in West Africa," &c.

Explorations of the Highlands of the Brazil; with a full account of the Gold and Diamond Mines; also, Canoeing down Fifteen Hundred Miles of the great River, Sao Francisco, from Sabarà to the Sea. In 2 vols. 8vo, with Map and Illustrations, 30s.

Letters from the Battle-fields of Paraguay. With Map and Illustrations, 18s.

Abeokuta; and an Exploration of the Cameroons Mountains. 2 vols. post 8vo, with Portrait of the Author, Map, and Illustrations. 25s.

The Nile Basin. With Map, &c. post 8vo, 7s. 6d.

A Mission to Geléle. Being a Three Months' Residence at the Court of Dahomé. In which are described the Manners and Customs of the Country, including the Human Sacrifice, &c. 2 vols., with Illustrations, 25s.

My Wanderings in West Africa; from Liverpool to Fernando Po. 2 vols. cr. 8vo, 21s.

Wit and Wisdom from West Africa; or a Book of Proverbial Philosophy, Idioms, Enigmas, and Laconisms. Compiled by RICHARD F. BURTON, author of "A Mission to Dahomé," "A Pilgrimage to El-Medinah and Meccah," &c. 12s. 6d.

WORKS BY GEORGE AUGUSTUS SALA.

My Diary in America in the Midst of War. In 2 vols. 8vo, 30s.

Notes and Sketches of the Paris Exhibition. 8vo, 15s.

From Waterloo to the Peninsula. 2 vols. 8vo, 24s.

Rome and Venice, with other Wanderings in Italy, in 1866–7. 8vo, 16s.

Dutch Pictures. With some Sketches in the Flemish Manner. 5s.

After Breakfast. A Sequel to "Breakfast in Bed." 2 vols. 21s.

Accepted Addresses. 1 vol. cr. 8vo, 5s.

TINSLEY BROTHERS, 18 CATHERINE STREET, STRAND.

History of France under the Bourbons, 1589-1830.
By CHARLES DUKE YONGE, Regius Professor, Queen's College, Belfast. In 4 vols. 8vo. Vols. I. and II. contain the Reigns of Henry IV., Louis XIII. and XIV.; Vols. III. and IV. contain the Reigns of Louis XV. and XVI. 3*l.*

The Regency of Anne of Austria, Queen of France,
Mother of Louis XIV. From Published and Unpublished Sources. With Portrait. By Miss FREER. 2 vols. 8vo, 30*s.*

The Married Life of Anne of Austria, Queen of
France, Mother of Louis XIV.; and the History of Don Sebastian, King of Portugal. Historical Studies. From numerous Unpublished Sources. By MARTHA WALKER FREER. 2 vols. 8vo, 30*s.*

The History of Monaco. By H. PEMBERTON. 12*s.*

The Great Country: Impressions of America. By
GEORGE ROSE, M.A. (ARTHUR SKETCHLEY). 8vo, 15*s.*

Biographies and Portraits of some Celebrated
People. By ALPHONSE DE LAMARTINE. 2 vols. 25*s.*

Memoirs of the Life and Reign of George III.
With Original Letters of the King and Other Unpublished MSS. By J. HENEAGE JESSE, author of "The Court of England under the Stuarts," &c. 3 vols. 8vo. £2 2*s.* Second Edition.

The Public Life of Lord Macaulay. By FREDERICK
ARNOLD, B.A. of Christ Church, Oxford. Post 8vo, 7*s.* 6*d.*

Memoirs of Sir George Sinclair, Bart., of Ulbster.
By JAMES GRANT, author of "The Great Metropolis," "The Religious Tendencies of the Times," &c. 8vo. With Portrait. 16*s.*

Memories of My Time; being Personal Remini-
scences of Eminent Men. By GEORGE HODDER. 8vo. 16*s.*

The Life of David Garrick. From Original Family
Papers, and numerous Published and Unpublished Sources. By PERCY FITZGERALD, M.A. 2 vols. 8vo, with Portraits. 36*s.*

The Life of Edmund Kean. From various Pub-
lished and Original Sources. By F. W. HAWKINS. In 2 vols. 8vo, 30*s.*

Johnny Robinson: The Story of the Childhood and
Schooldays of an "Intelligent Artisan." By the Author of "Some Habits and Customs of the Working Classes." 2 vols. 21*s.*

TINSLEY BROTHERS, 18 CATHERINE STREET, STRAND.

The Story of the Diamond Necklace. By HENRY
VIZETELLY. Illustrated with an exact representation of the Diamond Necklace, and a Portrait of the Countess de la Motte, engraved
on steel. 2 vols. post 8vo, 25s. Second Edition.

English Photographs. By an American. 8vo, 12s.

Travels in Central Africa, and Exploration of the
Western Nile Tributaries. By Mr. and Mrs. PETHERICK. With
Maps, Portraits, and numerous Illustrations. 2 vols. 8vo, 25s.

From Calcutta to the Snowy Range. By an OLD
INDIAN. With numerous coloured Illustrations. 14s.

Stray Leaves of Science and Folk-lore. By J. SCOF-
FERN, M.B. Lond. 8vo. 12s.

Three Hundred Years of a Norman House. With
Genealogical Miscellanies. By JAMES HANNAY, author of "A
Course of English Literature," "Satire and Satirists," &c. 12s.

The Religious Life of London. By J. EWING RITCHIE,
author of the "Night Side of London," &c. 8vo. 12s.

Religious Thought in Germany. By the TIMES
CORRESPONDENT at Berlin. Reprinted from the *Times.* 8vo. 12s.

Mornings of the Recess in 1861-4. Being a Series
of Literary and Biographical Papers, reprinted from the *Times*, by
permission, and revised by the Author. 2 vols. 21s.

The Schleswig-Holstein War. By EDWARD DICEY,
author of "Rome in 1860." 2 vols. 16s.

The Battle-fields of 1866. By EDWARD DICEY,
author of "Rome in 1860," &c. 12s.

From Sedan to Saarbrück, viâ Verdun, Gravelotte,
and Metz. By an Officer of the Royal Artillery. In one vol. 7s. 6d.

British Senators; or Political Sketches, Past and
Present. By J. EWING RITCHIE. Post 8vo, 10s. 6d.

Photographs of Paris Life; being a Record of
Politics, Art, Fashion, &c. By CHRONIQUEUSE. 7s. 6d.

Ten Years in Sarawak. By CHARLES BROOKE, the
"Tuanmudah" of Sarawak. With an Introduction by H. H. the
Rajah Sir JAMES BROOKE ; and numerous Illustrations. 2 vols. 25s.

Peasant Life in Sweden. By L. LLOYD, author
of "The Game Birds of Sweden," "Scandinavian Adventures," &c.
8vo. With Illustrations. 18s.

Hog Hunting in the East, and other Sports. By
Captain J. NEWALL, author of "The Eastern.Hunters." With numerous Illustrations. 8vo, 21s.

Shooting and Fishing in the Rivers, Prairies, and
Backwoods of North America. By B. H. REVOIL. 2 vols. 21s.

The Eastern Hunters. By Captain JAMES NEWALL.
8vo, with numerous Illustrations. 16s.

Fish Hatching; and the Artificial Culture of Fish.
By FRANK BUCKLAND. With 5 Illustrations. 5s.

The Open Air; or Sketches out of Town. By
JOSEPH VEREY. 1 vol.

Con Amore; or, Critical Chapters. By JUSTIN
MCCARTHY, author of "The Waterdale Neighbours." Post 8vo,
12s.

Murmurings in the May and Summer of Manhood:
O'Ruark's Bride, or the Blood-spark in the Emerald ; and Man's
Mission a Pilgrimage to Glory's Goal. By EDMUND FALCONER.
1 vol., 5s.

Poems. By EDMUND FALCONER. 1 vol., 5s.

Dante's Divina Commedia. Translated into English in the Metre and Triple Rhyme of the Original. By Mrs. RAM-
SAY. 3 vols. 18s.

The Gaming Table, its Votaries and Victims, in all
Countries and Times, especially in England and France. By ANDREW
STEINMETZ, Barrister-at-Law. 2 vols. 8vo. 31s.

Principles of Comedy and Dramatic Effect. By
PERCY FITZGERALD, author of "The Life of Garrick," &c. 8vo. 12s.

A Winter Tour in Spain. By the Author of "Altogether Wrong." 8vo, illustrated, 15s.

TINSLEY BROTHERS'
CHEAP EDITIONS OF POPULAR NOVELS.

By Mrs. HENRY WOOD, author of " East Lynne," &c.

The Red Court Farm. 6s.

A Life's Secret. 6s.

George Canterbury's Will. 6s.

Anne Hereford. 6s.

Elster's Folly. 6s.

St. Martin's Eve. 6s.

Mildred Arkell. 6s.

Trevlyn Hold. 6s.

By the Author of " Guy Livingstone."

Sword and Gown. 5s.

Barren Honour. 6s.

Brakespeare. 6s.

Maurice Dering. 6s.

Guy Livingstone. 5s.

Sans Merci. 6s.

Border and Bastille. 6s.

Also, now ready, uniform with the above,

A Life's Assize. By Mrs. J. H. RIDDELL, author of " Too Much Alone," " City and Suburb," " George Geith," &c. 6s.

A Righted Wrong. By EDMUND YATES. 6s.

Stretton. By HENRY KINGSLEY, author of " Geoffry Hamlyn," &c. 6s.

The Rock Ahead. By EDMUND YATES. 6s.

The Adventures of Dr. Brady. By W. H. RUSSELL, LL.D. 6s.

Black Sheep. By EDMUND YATES, author of " The Rock Ahead," &c. 6s.

Not Wisely, but Too Well. By the Author of " Cometh up as a Flower." 6s.

Miss Forrester. By the Author of "Archie Lovell," &c. 6s.

Recommended to Mercy. By the Author of " Sink or Swim ?" 6s.

Lizzie Lorton of Greyrigg. By Mrs. LYNN LINTON, author of " Sowing the Wind," &c. 6s.

The Seven Sons of Mammon. By G. A. SALA, author of " After Breakfast," &c. 6s.

The Cambridge Freshman: the Adventures of Mr. Golightly. By MARTIN LEGRAND. 1 vol., handsomely Illustrated. 6s.

TINSLEY BROTHERS' NEW NOVELS.

New Novel by Henry Kingsley.

The Harveys. By HENRY KINGSLEY, author of
"Old Margaret," "Hetty," "Geoffry Hamlyn," &c. 2 vols.

Henry Ancrum: a Tale of the last War in New
Zealand. 2 vols.

She was Young, and He was Old. 3 vols.

A Ready-made Family: or the Life and Adventures
of Julian Leep's Cherub. A Story. 3 vols.

Cecil's Tryst. By JAMES PAYN. 3 vols.

Love and Treason. By W. FREELAND. 3 vols.

Denison's Wife. By Mrs. ALEXANDER FRASER,
author of "Not while She lives," "Faithless; or the Loves of the
Period," &c. 2 vols.

Old Margaret. By HENRY KINGSLEY, author of
"Ravenshoe," "Geoffry Hamlyn," &c. 2 vols.

Two Plunges for a Pearl. By MORTIMER COLLINS,
author of "The Vivian Romance," &c. 3 vols.

Barbara Heathcote's Trial. By the Author of
"Nellie's Memories," &c. 3 vols.

Wide of the Mark. By the Author of "Recommended to Mercy," "Taken upon Trust," &c. 3 vols.

Bide Time and Tide. By J. T. NEWALL, author of
"The Gage of Honour," "The Eastern Hunters," &c. 3 vols.

The Scandinavian Ring. By JOHN POMEROY. 3 vols.

Tregarthen Hall. By JAMES GARLAND. 3 vols.

TINSLEY BROTHERS, 18 CATHERINE STREET, STRAND.

Title and Estate. By F. LANCASTER. 3 vols.

Hollowhill Farm. By JOHN EDWARDSON. 3 vols.

The Sapphire Cross: a Tale of Two Generations.
By G. M. FENN, author of "Bent, not Broken," &c. 3 vols.

Edith. By C. A. LEE. 2 vols.

Lady Judith. By JUSTIN McCARTHY, author of
"My Enemy's Daughter," "The Waterdale Neighbours," &c. 3 vols.

Only an Ensign. By JAMES GRANT, author of "The
Romance of War," "Lady Wedderburn's Wish," &c. 3 vols.

Old as the Hills. By DOUGLAS MOREY FORD. 3 vols.

Not Wooed, but Won. By the Author of "Lost
Sir Massingberd," "Found Dead," &c. 3 vols.

My Heroine. 1 vol.

The Prussian Spy. By V. VALMONT. 2 vols.

Sundered Lives. By WYBERT REEVE, author of the
Comedies of "Won at Last," "Not so Bad after all," &c. 3 vols.

The Nomads of the North: a Tale of Lapland. By
J. LOVEL HADWEN. 1 vol.

Family Pride. By the Author of "Olive Varcoe,"
"Simple as a Dove," &c. 3 vols.

Fair Passions; or the Setting of the Pearls. By the
Hon. Mrs. PIGOTT CARLETON. 3 vols.

Harry Disney: an Autobiography. Edited by
ATHOLL DE WALDEN. 3 vols.

Desperate Remedies. 3 vols.

The Foster Sisters. By EDMOND BRENAN LOUGHNAN.
3 vols.

TINSLEY BROTHERS, 18 CATHERINE STREET, STRAND.

Only a Commoner. By HENRY MORFORD. 3 vols.

Madame la Marquise. By the Author of "Dacia
Singleton," "What Money Can't Do," &c. 3 vols.

Clara Delamaine. By A. W. CUNNINGHAM. 3 vols.

Sentenced by Fate. By Miss EDGCOMBE. 3 vols.

Fairly Won. By Miss H. S. ENGSTRÖM. 3 vols.

Joshua Marvel. By B. L. FARJEON, author of
"Grif." 3 vols.

Blanche Seymour. 3 vols.

By Birth a Lady. By G. M. FENN, author of
"Mad," "Webs in the Way," &c. 3 vols.

A Life's Assize. By Mrs. J. H. RIDDELL, author
of "George Geith," "City and Suburb," "Too much Alone," &c.
3 vols.

Gerald Hastings. By the Author of "No Appeal,"
&c. 3 vols.

Monarch of Mincing-Lane. By WILLIAM BLACK,
author of "In Silk Attire," "Kilmeny," &c. 3 vols.

The Golden Bait. By H. HOLL, author of "The
King's Mail," &c. In 3 vols.

Like Father, like Son. By the Author of "Lost
Sir Massingberd," &c. 3 vols.

Beyond these Voices. By the EARL OF DESART,
author of "Only a Woman's Love," &c. 3 vols.

The Queen's Sailors. A Nautical Novel. By ED-
WARD GREEY. 3 vols.

Bought with a Price. By the Author of "Golden
Pippin," &c. 1 vol.

TINSLEY BROTHERS, 18 CATHERINE STREET, STRAND.

The Florentines: a Story of Home-life in Italy.
By the COUNTESS MARIE MONTEMERLI, author of " Four Months in a Garibaldian Hospital," &c. 3 vols.

The Inquisitor. By WILLIAM GILBERT, author of
" Doctor Austin's Guests," &c. 3 vols.

Falsely True. By Mrs. CASHEL HOEY, author of
" A House of Cards," &c. In 3 vols.

After Baxtow's Death. By MORLEY FARROW, author
of " No Easy Task," &c. 3 vols.

Hearts and Diamonds. By ELIZABETH P. RAMSAY,
3 vols.

The Bane of a Life. By THOMAS WRIGHT (the
Journeyman Engineer), author of " Some Habits and Customs of the Working Classes," &c. 3 vols.

Robert Lynne. By MARY BRIDGMAN. 2 vols.

Baptised with a Curse. By EDITH S. DREWRY.
3 vols.

Brought to Book. By HENRY SPICER, Esq. 2 vols.

Fenacre Grange. By LANGFORD CECIL. 3 vols.

Schooled with Briars: a Story of To-day. 1 vol.

A Righted Wrong. By EDMUND YATES, author of
" Black Sheep," &c. 3 vols.

Gwendoline's Harvest. By the Author of " Lost
Sir Massingberd," " Found Dead," &c. 2 vols.

A Fool's Paradise. By THOMAS ARCHER, author of
" Strange Work," &c. 3 vols.

George Canterbury's Will. By Mrs. HENRY WOOD,
author of " East Lynne," &c. 3 vols.

TINSLEY BROTHERS, 18 CATHERINE STREET, STRAND.

Gold and Tinsel. By the Author of "Ups and Downs of an Old Maid's Life." 3 vols.

Sidney Bellew. A Sporting Story. By FRANCIS FRANCIS. 2 vols.

Grif; a Story of Australian Life. By B. LEOPOLD FARJEON. 2 vols.

Not while She Lives. By the Author of "Faithless; or the Loves of the Period." 2 vols.

A Double Secret and Golden Pippin. By JOHN POMEROY. 3 vols.

Wee Wific. By ROSA NOUCHETTE CAREY, author of "Nellie's Memories." 3 vols.

Oberon Spell. By EDEN ST. LEONARDS. 3 vols.

Daisie's Dream. By the Author of "Recommended to Mercy," &c. 3 vols.

Heathfield Hall; or Prefatory Life. A Youthful Reminiscence. By HANS SCHREIBER, author of "Nicknames at the Playingfield College," &c. 10s. 6d.

Phœbe's Mother. By LOUISA ANN MEREDITH, author of "My Bush Friends in Tasmania." 2 vols.

Strong Hands and Steadfast Hearts. By the Countess von BOTHMER. 3 vols.

The Lily and the Rose. By G. H. HARWOOD. 3 vols.

Love Stories of the English Watering-Places. 3 vols.

My Enemy's Daughter. By JUSTIN McCARTHY, author of "The Waterdale Neighbours," "Paul Massie," &c. 3 vols.

A County Family. By the Author of "Lost Sir Massingberd," &c. 3 vols.

TINSLEY BROTHERS, 18 CATHERINE STREET, STRAND.

Only a Woman's Love. By the EARL OF DESART. 2 vols.

Up and Down the World. By the Author of "Never—for Ever." 3 vols.

Lost Footsteps. By JOSEPH VEREY. 3 vols.

The Gage of Honour. By Captain J. T. NEWALL. 3 vols.

Twice Refused. By CHARLES E. STIRLING. 2 vols.

Fatal Zero. By the Author of "Polly," &c. 2 vols.

Stretton. By HENRY KINGSLEY, author of "Geoffry Hamlyn," &c. 3 vols.

False Colours. By ANNIE THOMAS (Mrs. PENDER CUDLIP), author of "Denis Donne." 3 vols.

In Silk Attire. By WILLIAM BLACK, author of "Love or Marriage?" 3 vols. Second Edition.

All but Lost. By G. A. HENTY, author of "The March to Magdala." 3 vols.

A London Romance. By CHARLES H. ROSS. 3 vols.

Home from India. By JOHN POMEROY. 2 vols.

John Twiller: a Romance of the Heart. By D. STARKEY, LL.D. 1 vol.

The Doctor of Beauweir. By WILLIAM GILBERT, author of "Shirley Hall Asylum," "Dr. Austin's Guests," &c. &c. 2 vols.

Mad: a Story of Dust and Ashes. By GEORGE MANVILLE FENN, author of "Bent, not Broken." 3 vols.

Buried Alone. By a New Writer. 1 vol.

TINSLEY BROTHERS, 18 CATHERINE STREET, STRAND.

Nellie's Memories: a Domestic Story. By ROSA NOUCHETTE CAREY. 3 vols.

Clarissa. By SAMUEL RICHARDSON. Edited by E. S. DALLAS, author of "The Gay Science," &c. 3 vols.

Love or Marriage? By WILLIAM BLACK. 3 vols.

John Haller's Niece. By the Author of "Never—for Ever." 3 vols.

Neighbours and Friends. By the Hon. Mrs. HENRY WEYLAND CHETWYND, author of "Three Hundred a Year." 3 vols.

Martyrs to Fashion. By JOSEPH VEREY. 3 vols.

A House of Cards. By Mrs. CASHEL HOEY. 3 vols.

Out of the Meshes. 3 vols.

Wild as a Hawk. By Mrs. MACQUOID, author of "Hester Kirton," &c. 3 vols.

Diana Gay. By PERCY FITZGERALD. 3 vols.

Giant Despair. By MORLEY FARROW. 3 vols.

Francesca's Love. By Mrs. EDWARD PULLEYNE. 3 vols.

Polly: a Village Portrait. 2 vols.

TINSLEY BROTHERS, 18 CATHERINE STREET, STRAND.

www.ingramcontent.com/pod-product-compliance
Lightning Source LLC
Chambersburg PA
CBHW030730280326
41926CB00086B/1050